KINGDOM OF HEAVEN™

Kingdom of Heaven™

The Ridley Scott Film and the History Behind the Story

Introduction by Ridley Scott

Newmarket Press
New York

Edited by DIANA LANDAU *Designed by* TIMOTHY SHANER
Additional writing by NANCY FRIEDMAN

This book is published in the United States of America.

ISBN 1-55704-708-1 Custom Edition

Library of Congress Cataloging-in-Publication Data available upon request.

QUANTITY PURCHASES
Companies, professional groups, clubs, and other organizations may qualify for special terms when ordering quantities of this title. For information or to obtain our catalog, write Special Sales Department, Newmarket Press, 18 East 48th Street, New York, NY 10017; call (212) 832-3575; fax (212) 832-3629; or e-mail info@newmarketpress.com.

www.newmarketpress.com

Manufactured in the United States of America.

Contents

Timberland

Introduction

Keys to the Kingdom

by Ridley Scott

At this moment—about two months away from delivering a finished movie—I'm in London, working with my colleagues in visual effects and editing to prepare a cut for previewing in mid-December. By early January it will be "locked" and ready for scoring. We're working fast, which I tend to do, but everything is going terrifically well, and I'm very excited about this film.

People who come to see *Kingdom of Heaven* will discover a moment in history that isn't well known. When one thinks of the Crusades, one generally imagines pitched battles between knights and Saracens, or endless sieges of forgotten fortresses. There will be plenty of fighting on the screen, for sure—we've created some impressive images of massive fields of battle with thousands of people (not all of them real) and huge medieval war machines that are completely real, built from scratch of heavy timbers and metal. There are siege towers and catapults that were carefully researched and constructed to fit with the era.

This is something I enjoy doing, and for me

LEFT: Ridley Scott and Ghassan Massoud as Saladin on the Jerusalem palace set with a bejeweled prop Cross, the ultimate Crusader symbol. The True Cross was said to have been captured during the Battle of Hattin, 1187.

it's more or less par for the course. I'm known for creating worlds on film, and I like to get into the research and the fine details. How do you re-create a particular situation in a certain century? That's part of the fascination of the job. And I admit I'm especially taken with those great contraptions that hurl heavy objects long distances. It probably goes back to a childhood game I played growing up in England, and which is still played, called Conkers. You have a horse chestnut dangling from a length of string, and you try to slingshot the chestnut so that

it hits your opponent's and cracks it. I was quite competitive at this and used to cheat, I'm afraid, by baking my chestnut in the oven until it was very hard, then polishing it with bootblack so it looked shiny and new. Then I'd have this perfectly lethal missile, like granite on a string; the others would be mystified when it smashed everything in sight. The trebuchets we built for the film were a bit like giant conkers, with an arm that pivots 56 feet and can sling 100 pounds of rock about 400 meters.

Anyway, I hope people enjoy that part as much as I did. But warfare is fairly predictable in a Crusades movie. What's unusual about this one is that our story offered the chance to show not just war but an attempt at peace. I always try to do something a little surprising—that's the target of drama, isn't it? You're trying to surprise the audience. So where people might assume war and bloodbath, we're coming at it from a different angle.

The period we are focused on is a brief era of truce that occurred between the Second and Third Crusades. I'd always wanted to make a movie about knights and medieval times, the Crusades especially. It was our scriptwriter, Bill Monahan, who came up with this period when the two cultures—Christian and Muslim—stood at peace, however uneasy and brief. The truce was maintained by two remarkable leaders, King Baldwin IV, who ruled the Latin Kingdom of Jerusalem, and the great Saracen general Saladin. Reading the exchanges that took place between these two, one is struck by the fact that they obviously held great respect for each other. There is no escaping the parallels with our time, when leaders who try to make peace are admired, but their efforts so often are subverted by more radical factions.

We set out to tell a terrific story from a supremely dramatic age—not to make a documentary or a piece that aims to moralize or propagandize. But since our subject is the clash of these two civilizations, and we are now living in the post-9/11 world, *Kingdom of Heaven* will inevitably be looked at from that perspective. We did make some conscious choices about the values expressed through the story, beginning with the central situation of two leaders trying to serve their own people and their sense of mission, while exercising a degree of tolerance of the "other."

Above: Concept art for a Saracen flag created by Jim Stanes bearing the motto "There is no success except through God."
Right: Orlando Bloom as a blacksmith turned Crusader, wearing his Army of Jerusalem livery.

Beyond that, certain values clearly are embodied in the central character of Balian, an innately good man and a seeker. Though he becomes a knight in the film, he already was the kind of person a knight was supposed to be: valorous in battle and honorable in personal conduct. He goes through a hard journey and various temptations, as heroes tend to do, but at the end of the day we want our heroes to emerge relatively pure, as someone who is fair and good and does the right thing. This may make me sound like a Boy Scout, but a little bit of Boy Scout would be very useful today. Chivalry is just good behavior; it's quite simple, really, yet we don't seem to be able to apply it.

But making a successful drama can't be all about high ideals or superb filmcraft. Working on a large canvas as we are, there's always the danger that the characters can get swamped. I've always tried to make sure there is a strong personal story within the big frame. Pulling this off is partly a matter of experience; also of having good collaborators. My model is David Lean, whose characters never got lost in the proscenium, and that's all to do with the screenplay. Bill Monahan's screenplay for *Kingdom* is one of the best I've ever worked with—it gives me everything. It gives me the canvas and the characters.

Then of course you need a great cast, actors who are strong enough to hold their own amid all the trappings and not seem hopelessly out of place in a period piece. We were incredibly fortunate in our cast, from Orlando Bloom and Eva Green, our leads, to great supporting performances by people like Liam Neeson, Jeremy Irons, David Thewlis, and Ghassan Massoud as Saladin.

You light and shoot the performances in ways that focus attention on the story lines. And down the line, in the post-production moves we are making now, you work with editing rhythms, sound, and scoring to make the interpersonal drama as powerful as the big action.

But mainly it's in the story: what happens to the characters and how they respond. It's been said that the medieval mind was very different from ours, to the point where we cannot hope to identify with the people of that time or understand their motivations. I don't necessarily agree with that. They may have faced very different challenges and lived with a level of violence we can hardly imagine. But even though it's based in history, a lot of the film's emotional territory will be familiar ground for us. It comes right from the heart in terms of who the characters are, the central personalities that run through the story and make its world evolve and dissolve.

It begins with Balian, a man who has lost everything worth living for. His child dies, his wife becomes so depressed that she commits suicide, and because the church hadn't outgrown this barbarous custom, she is considered damned and denied burial in holy ground. So he's a man in total bewilderment about his religious roots and what to do with his life. One motive for joining the Crusaders and going to Jerusalem is to redeem her soul, but the journey is also a kind of redemption for him—he is seeking forgiveness for sins of his own. So it's a spiritual journey, but also one that serves to demonstrate his inner nobility by how he responds to life-threatening and soul-threatening challenges.

The knight Godfrey is a good man but more worldly than religious. He talks about the opportunities the Holy Land presents, and he talks about an ideology that's based on right action and common sense. Both of which we could use a lot more of these days.

Then the princess Sibylla: her story is very specific to the period but its human tragedy can speak to anyone. She is very close to her brother, the king, but since he has been destroyed by leprosy, she can't bear to touch him. She is attracted to Balian, but for the sake of the kingdom she must remain married to a man she loathes.

Jeremy Irons is terrific as the king's chief advisor, Tiberias: a man who has served his government faithfully but finds himself worn down by the effort of peace-keeping; he has a diminishing itinerary of passion for the job he is doing and for being in the Holy Land at all.

I wanted people to see events from the Muslims' point of view as well, and the way to do that was to develop strong, multidimensional characters on that side. Especially Saladin, as played by Ghassan Massoud, a wonderful Syrian actor. I felt it was important to use Muslim actors to play Muslim characters. You see Saladin in private moments; you see his leadership, how he tries to keep the peace as long as he can. He was under pressure from his people, and on the other side there was the radical faction of Templars and other knights—what we might call the right wing or Christian fundamentalists of their day. And he is a man with a strong sense of his destiny.

You might do a magnificent job of creating an unfamiliar world—a far place, a far-off time, or both—with the most skilled filmmakers and the best technology available. But at the end of the day, you have to make sure that world is inhabited by people whose lives and fates we care about and whose story has something to say to us. The Crusades were a sometimes glorious, often tragic, and world-shaping series of events that are still having an impact on events today. I hope that in opening a cinematic window on that time, we're doing the job that good drama is meant to do: to excite our emotions, stir our souls, and make us think, all at once.

Above: Ridley Scott directs Nasser Memarzia, who plays the Muslim Grandee, in the caravan attack filmed near Ait Ben Haddou.

Part 1

Kingdoms in the Holy Land

The Crusades and the Film Story

Moments in Time

"You've written 'EXT. JERUSALEM. DAY' at a table in your garage, which is where I wrote the film, and two years later you're standing in the Sahara, where Ridley Scott has built maybe the largest free-standing set in the history of the movies. Listening to Jeremy Irons cover a line of dialogue you've written. Even when I saw armies, helicopters, and the Jerusalem set, or was driving through the desert looking at knights riding along a ridgeline, I think I was still blocking things out: it was all so huge, so gratifying, an awfully impressive situation."

This was the situation in which screenwriter William Monahan found himself in the spring of 2004, during principal photography in Morocco for *Kingdom of Heaven*. Behind this moment were many years of dreaming, scribbling, research, and toil; more than a year ahead lay the movie's release date of May 2005.

As with all major film projects, this moment represented a complex intersection of individual talents and histories. At the nexus of this crossroads (a key image in the film story!) stands director-producer Ridley Scott, wholly in his element as the commander of vast forces generating an epic period film production. Monahan's words had given shape and substance to Scott's glimmer of an idea for a film on knighthood and its ultimate mission: the Crusades; had enabled him literally to see the characters and story as they would come to exist on the screen.

Around Scott—on the sets in Morocco and in offices or workshops in Los Angeles, London, Madrid, Rome, Bombay, and Shanghai—are thousands more, all indispensable in their way to bringing the movie to this moment and beyond. They include executives at the Twentieth Century Fox studio, who set such projects in motion and bring them to the public; producers who arrange for personnel, materiél, and funds to get to the right places at the right times; production heads who have learned from experience to read Scott's mind and interpret his constant flow of drawings to create sets, costumes, camera angles, and film effects. Ultimately drawn into the circle were seamstresses

sewing crosses onto flags in India, armorers creating chainmail from miracle plastics in China, and a crew close to a thousand strong, composed of technicians from all over North America and Europe, as well as 400-plus Moroccans working in that country's film industry.

Not to mention the talent in front of the camera: from thousands of expert horse and camel riders, to stuntmen and -women, to the featured actors: a truly international cast that includes distinguished veterans (Jeremy Irons, Liam Neeson, Brendan Gleeson); stars from the world of Arab stage and film who will be seen in a major Holly-wood release for the first time (Ghassan Massoud as Saladin, Alexander Siddig as Imad, Khaled 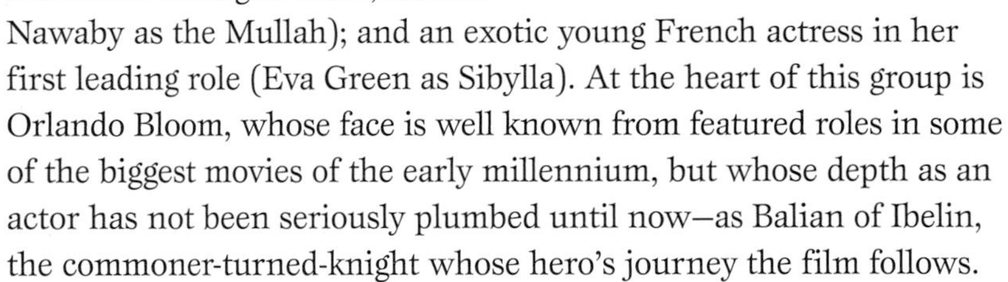Nawaby as the Mullah); and an exotic young French actress in her first leading role (Eva Green as Sibylla). At the heart of this group is Orlando Bloom, whose face is well known from featured roles in some of the biggest movies of the early millennium, but whose depth as an actor has not been seriously plumbed until now—as Balian of Ibelin, the commoner-turned-knight whose hero's journey the film follows.

Indeed, Orlando Bloom carries a big responsibility in this film. Balian is the latest incarnation of Ridley Scott's archetypal hero: a gifted and extraordinary man (or woman), though not one born to power, caught up in great events—a sympathetic character who gives audiences a place to focus their attention and emotions within a cinematic canvas of epic scope. Even more, a character who comes through hardship or tragedy to emerge as a real hero, someone who sets an example by taking a stand and refusing to be moved off it. Maximus, the up-from-the-ranks Roman general turned rebel in *Gladiator* is one example; Deckard, the blade runner with a conscience, is another; as is Ripley in the original *Alien*.

You have to make sure that the world you create is inhabited by people whose lives and fates we care about.

– Ridley Scott

A Hero's Journey

Balian, as *Kingdom of Heaven* opens, is a young blacksmith in medieval France, circa 1180s—"an artificer," as Scott describes him, who in another era would be a talented engineer. With his baby's death and his wife's suicide, he has lost his family, but he soon meets a man who will change his life: the true knight Godfrey of Ibelin, a Crusader on his way back to the Holy Land after a visit home. Through various circumstances, Balian joins Godfrey on his journey, and like many other crusaders finds a fate he never imagined in the Latin Kingdom of Jerusalem.

The new land where Balian finds himself—Palestine and Syria between the Second and Third Crusades—is a world of great sweetness and great peril. Sweet to Balian are the exotic tastes of the East, the novel experience of leading other men in his new domain, and especially the romantic attentions of Princess Sibylla, sister to the dying King of Jerusalem. Perilous is the whole situation of Christian Jerusalem and the European knights in their outposts strung along

PRECEDING PAGES: Crowds gather at a well in one of the courtyards of the Jerusalem set. ABOVE: Location scouting in the Tissa Dunes. Just inland from the town of Essaouira in Morocco, this is where Balian's encounter with Imad and the Saracen knight was filmed. OVERLEAF: Orlando Bloom as Balian with Godfrey, played by Liam Neeson, on the Messina set.

the Mediterranean at this time, as the Saracen commander Saladin expands his power. Saladin and the young leper king, Baldwin IV, have forged a tenuous truce, which is ever threatened by extremists on both sides. Perilous, too, is Balian's involvement with Sibylla, married to one of those extremists, Guy de Lusignan, who craves the crown for himself.

In another moment of filming Monahan describes: (INT. PALACE. DAY)–Guy's accomplice, Reynald of Chatillon, has been hauled before the king's minister (Jeremy Irons as Tiberias), accused of provoking conflict by raiding a Muslim caravan. "Who says I raid?" blusters Reynald, and Tiberias looks up from his desk and replies, "This witness, all Jerusalem, Holy God, and me!" Says Monahan: "This was the first time as a dramatist that I'd ever seen a solitary line of mine performed, and the guy saying the line was Jeremy Irons, in a palace in Spain, in a film directed by Ridley Scott. I had to go sit in the garden and think about this."

The rest of Monahan's tale unfolds around Balian's quest to uphold his personal understanding of knightly honor as he navigates this medieval minefield, and his practical gifts as a craftsman and leader during Saladin's climactic siege of Jerusalem.

Kingdom's Roots

By the time these moments play out, the arc traversed by this film production is far advanced. The production sprang into action early in 2003, when Scott told Twentieth Century Fox that *Kingdom of Heaven* was going to be his next picture. Scott's chief lieutenants and creative collaborators, including producers Lisa Ellzey, Branko Lustig, and Terry Needham; production designer Arthur Max; cinematographer John Mathieson; and costume designer Janty Yates, were mobilized to begin their work of scouting, research, and assembling resources. By the end of that year sets were rising in northern and southern Spain, and near Ourzazate, Scott's favorite Morocco location; by spring 2004, the film's early scenes, set in a European winter, had already been shot in the foothills of the Pyrénées. Those sets would soon come down.

But to trace this film project to its origins, keep backtracking. Scott conceived a wish to explore knighthood on film as much as 18

The Reel Crusades

The Crusades, the Middle Ages, and knight errantry have been mined by moviemakers almost since actor first mounted horse. Here is an eclectic selection.

The Crusades (1935)
Cecil B. DeMille's take on King Richard and the Third Crusade (1190–1192), starring Henry Wilcoxon. Loretta Young as Berengaria, Princess of Navarre, visits Saladin's harem; Ian Keith is the first of many non-Arab actors to play Saladin. Said Pauline Kael, "DeMille willfully garbled every single character and incident."

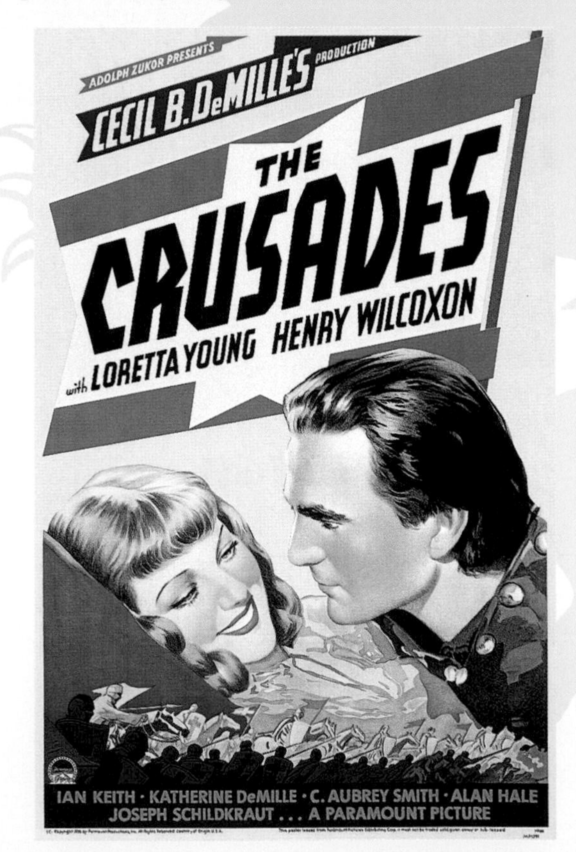

Alexander Nevsky (1938)
Sergei Eisenstein's great film about Russian warriors beating back a German invasion in the 13th century, with a score by Prokofiev.

Ivanhoe (1952)
First of several adaptations of the Walter Scott romance, with Robert Taylor as the noble knight and Elizabeth Taylor as Rebecca (a rare movie appearance for a medieval Jewish character).

King Richard and the Crusaders (1954)
Based on Walter Scott's *The Talisman*, this has a disguised Saladin (Rex Harrison!) sneaking into the Christian camp to cure Richard Lionheart. Few redeeming values.

The Seventh Seal (1957)
Ingmar Bergman's classic, set in 14th-century Sweden, about a knight (Max von Sydow) returning from a crusade and playing a chess game with Death. More a philosophical than a historical exercise.

The Mighty Crusaders (1957)
Italian director Carlo Ludovico Bragaglia adapts Renaissance poet Torquato Tasso's epic *Jerusalem Delivered* on the exploits of Godfrey of Boulogne in the First Crusade.

Knights of the Black Cross (1960)
Directed by Aleksander Ford, this Polish epic is set at the turn of the 14th century and focuses on events leading to the Battle of Grunwald.

The story involves a Polish nobleman whose daughter is kidnapped by the Teutonic Knights, one of the religious/military orders.

El Cid (1961)
Anthony Mann's respectable retelling of the legend of El Cid, the hero who drives the Moors from 11th-century Spain. Charlton Heston is Rodrigo Diaz (El Cid) and Sophia Loren is his love interest; a Miklos Rozsa score.

El Naser Salah el Dine (1963)
In this Egyptian movie Saladin is presented as a prototype of Gamel Abdul Nasser, in calling for Arab unity to expel western intruders.

The War Lord (1965)
Adaptation of Leslie Stevens novel revolves around the custom of *droigt de seigneur*: a knight may ravish another man's bride. (*Braveheart* used the same theme.) Charlton Heston, in a bowl-cut hairdo, is the knight.

The Lion in Winter (1968)
Highly entertaining, reasonably accurate portrait of family life with the Plantagenets: Henry II (Peter O'Toole), Eleanor of Aquitaine (Katherine Hepburn), and their sons; Anthony Hopkins is a sullen Richard. After one knockdown battle with Henry, Eleanor wryly observes, "Every family has its up and downs."

Andrei Rublev (1969)
Russian director Andrei Tarkovsky's masterpiece depicts 15th-century feudal wars (Russia was a few centuries behind Europe) through the life of the title character, a visionary icon painter.

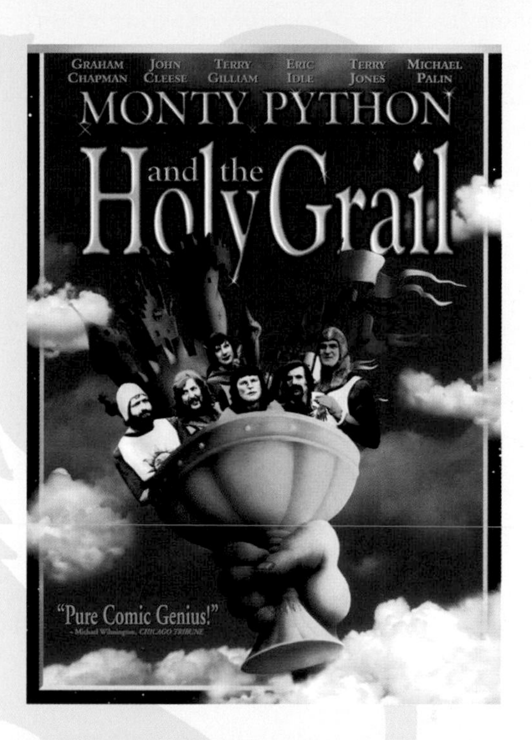

Monty Python and the Holy Grail (1975)
The Pythons have their merry, bloodthirsty way with Arthurian legend, monastic life, witch trials, and the Black Death. Codirector Terry Jones went on to write a companion book to the BBC/A&E *Crusades* series.

Lionheart (1987)
Eric Stoltz as the young French knight who leads the ill-fated Childrens' Crusade in the 12th century.

A Knight's Tale (2001)
Brian Helgeland depicts the jousting circuit to the strains of "We Will Rock You." Heath Ledger is the young stud knight; Paul Bettany plays a feckless Chaucer.

years ago. The impulse was a natural one, given the characters that interest him. Centuries of myth have coalesced around the knight, and while the image of a solitary warrior off on a noble quest, bound by oaths of chivalry and purity, owes much to the 19th-century imagination, the reality is fascinating enough. Knights were the dominant military force in Europe for five centuries, often doubling as landholder, defender of the faith, and/or troubadour. They probably exerted more influence on history than other other type of soldier.

"Historically, the knight—like the cowboy or more recently the policeman—represents a person on the leading edge of his culture at a particular time," Scott says. "These figures have always given us great opportunities to tell stories that carry the attributes of a hero. And one of the most important is that the character carries with him his own degrees of fairness, faithfulness, and chivalry. What it's really about is right action."

Scott cites as a key influence Ingmar Bergman's *The Seventh Seal*, with its mysterious tale of a knight returning from his crusade and playing a chess game with Death. "I think the knight has always been in my sights since I was brought up on a diet of Ingmar Bergman. And of course the Japanese knights in Kurosawa have always represented something that I would try to do as a film some day." The visual spectacle of warfare in Akira Kurosawa's films about medieval Japan—the colorful banners in snapping ranks, the cavalry charges, the drama of sieges—stirred Scott as well. He puts his own visual stamp on those elements in *Kingdom of Heaven*.

The director also admires a pair of classic Russian films that deal with knightly warfare and the medieval milieu: Sergei Eisenstein's *Alexander Nevsky* and Andre Tarkovsky's *Andrei Rublev*—the latter actually focusing on the spiritual struggles of the great icon painter Rublev in 15th-century Russian history, a period marked by Tatar invasions and endless fighting among rival princes.

From knights to the Crusades was a very short step. "From what sort of a medieval, dark ages story could this character of a knight emerge?" went Scott's thinking. "What started to visit in terms of an idea was: if you're going to do a story about a knight, you'd better do it

RIGHT: Illustration from Eugène Violett-le-Duc's Encyclopédie Médiévale, *1854, shows siege towers and catapults being used in an attack on a medieval city.*

about the most significant period in that history. The Crusades spanned over 200 years and gave rise to so many astounding stories–besides all the cinematic possibilities of the Holy Land setting and the clash of cultures between Europe and the East. It was the obvious target."

But which story? As a first step toward realizing his germ of an idea, Scott early in 2001 asked Lisa Ellzey, president of Scott Free in Los Angeles, to start scouting for a story and a writer who could bring forth situations and characters he might want to film. No problem, she thought. "We met with a few writers to discuss the idea. Some did quite a bit of research but lacked compelling story lines. Some found the topic too dicey."

That autumn Ellzey read a spec screenplay called *Tripoli* by a new writer, William Monahan, and it struck her as possibly suitable for Scott to direct–but it also occurred to her that Monahan would be a strong choice for a Crusades screenplay. "In *Tripoli*, Monahan was able to tell a complex story about two sides of a political/military/cultural struggle while avoiding black-and-white clichés."

She called Scott, who was wrapping principal photography for *Black Hawk Down* in Morocco, and pitched him the story. "He turned me down flat. He was ready to get the hell out of the desert, and I was asking him to consider another story in the same setting! I implored him to read the script anyway, as a writing sample for the Crusades project." Less than a week later, he called her to say he loved *Tripoli*, might direct it, and wanted to meet with Monahan.

Soon after, Twentieth Century Fox acquired the project with Scott informally attached–an arrangement that was firmed up after Monahan made some revisions in response to notes from Scott, Fox, and others. *Tripoli* came within a whisker of going into full production, but was derailed late in the process due to cast scheduling conflicts. Scott plans to revive it at the next opportunity.

Tripoli shared key traits with the future *Kingdom of Heaven,* no doubt one reason it appealed to Scott. He says, "It was a very interesting script: again a historical tale and very political–set on the Barbary Coast of North Africa in 1803, at the time of Thomas Jefferson. It was romantic but well documented, carefully and beautifully seen, as only a good historian or a great journalist could do." And each has a protagonist who undertakes a perilous journey.

As many have observed, the central characters in Scott's films tend to share a certain ethos and spirit. There is a code that the heroes try to live by, notwithstanding the apparent absence of any kind of moral structure in the film's universe. (The worlds of *Alien, Blade Runner*, and *Gladiator*'s Roman Empire come to mind.) In fact, it's usually quite the opposite: often a structure of evil or misfortune is arrayed against them. These are harsh worlds, and the heroes have to survive in them.

It goes without saying that for Monahan, the chance to have Ridley Scott direct his first film script was almost too good to be true. "Ridley's early film *The Duellists* is an extraordinary work and actually inspired me to write *Tripoli*, also set in Napoleonic times, as a film drama rather than a novel. So our coming together was extremely fortuitous."

The crucial date in *Kingdom of Heaven*'s genesis fell in November 2001. Script work on *Tripoli* was under way, and Scott arranged to meet Monahan for the first time in New York, where the director was promoting *Black Hawk Down*. "We talked about *Tripoli*, of course," recalls Scott, "but then I started to talk about general subjects and material. Of course the idea of a knight came up. Something that would happen in that vague period we term 'medieval.' We discussed every director: Kurosawa, Eisenstein. Bill said, 'Let me think about it'–and that's how it went."

Monahan remembers the morning in vivid detail: "In the course of the conversation, perhaps towards its end, he asked me if I had anything about the Crusades. I was still barely processing the idea that Ridley Scott was going to direct a film I had written, and he's asking if I might have another film. The nightmare would have been that I'd have nothing–but I did have something. I thought immediately of the Latin Kingdom of Jerusalem, and the leper king Baldwin IV."

Monahan refrained from launching into specifics on the spot, but went home, checked his sources, and about a month later outlined the story to Scott and Ellzey. By January 2002, after several more story meetings, Scott had requested that Fox make a blind script commitment for this new project on the Crusades; Hutch Parker, president of Twentieth Century Fox, certified the deal. Recalls Scott: "At a certain point Bill came in and pitched the story, pretty much as it came to be written: of Balian learning who his natural father is and

his journey through many misadventures to arrive in the Holy Land; all the events as they were ultimately embodied in the script. I said, 'It sounds like a hell of a movie; why don't you write it?' And he did."

Nearly a year later, in November, Monahan delivered a 180-page draft script for *Kingdom of Heaven* to Scott Free. This was another critical juncture: *Tripoli* had just been pulled from production, and Scott was set to begin filming another project for Sony. But he read Monahan's script immediately.

"Ridley called me the day after Thanksgiving and told me this would be his next film," says Ellzey. "From that moment he became a force of nature, prepared to demolish anything in his path to get the movie made. He willed *Kingdom of Heaven* into existence." Seven months later, after working with Monahan to cut 30 pages from the script, Scott formally presented it to Fox with a cover letter declaring, "This is the best script I have ever developed." Which brings our tale back to the moment when he put his team on notice, and it was full steam ahead. Scott undertook to deliver the film on a short schedule. The preliminary work on *Tripoli* actually helped effect this, as he was able to take advantage of location scouting and other resources identified for the earlier project.

In constructing the script, Monahan notes, "I proceeded with more or less what had first flashed into my head when Ridley asked about medieval knights and the Crusades. It was an extraordinary opportunity, which only Ridley could have made possible. My working for him is such a lovely piece of artistic luck that sometimes it seems almost supernaturally preordained."

On that November day when Scott and Monahan met in New York and raised the subject of the Crusades, the reek of the 9/11 attacks still hung in the air. Though it didn't enter their discussion then, the coming of *jihad* to America surely had an impact on how they would respond to the subject. Both men recognized that their chosen material, which had inspired earlier generations of filmmakers and storytellers with its romance and pageantry, its stirring warfare and epic sweep, would take on a different dimension for today's movie audiences. The struggle between Christendom and Islam a millennium ago would be seen, for better or worse, in a sobering new light.

Being who they were, they didn't shy from the task.

The Lords of Outremer

"*Deus lo volt*—God wills it!"

The crowd of clergymen, knights, and noblemen, assembled in a huge field in Clermont, France, roars with a single voice. It is a cold late-November day in 1095, but their collective fervor burns away the chill. They have just heard a speech that stuns and then galvanizes them–a call to arms unlike any they have ever heard.

The speaker is Pope Urban II, by birth a French nobleman. He speaks not in Church Latin but in French, the language of daily life. And his words are nothing short of incendiary.

"Distressing news has come to us," he begins, "that the people of the Persian kingdom, an accursed race, a race utterly alienated from God...has [sic] invaded Christian lands and devastated them with sword, pillage, and fire." Urban goes on to describe in graphic–and wholly inaccurate–detail the desecration of Christian holy sites, the torture and murder of innocent men, "the abominable rape of women." And then he sounds his battle cry.

"Who shall avenge these wrongs, who shall recover these lands, if not you?" Urban challenges the crowd. "Oh, most valiant knights, descendants of unconquerable ancestors, remember the courage of your forefathers and do not dishonor them!"

His audience murmurs excitedly. Can the pope actually be urging them to kill? Is killing not a mortal sin, a sin for which Christian knights–who are trained to fight wars yet know that Christ taught his followers to "turn the other cheek"–can never completely repent?

But Urban has an answer. "If you must have blood," he says, "bathe in the blood of infidels. Soldiers of Hell, become soldiers of the living God!"

It is a revolutionary war cry, with its promise of eternal reward

Right: Battle between Saracens and Christians during the Crusades, from Chroniques des empereurs *by David Aubert, 1462.*

and redemption. The crowd shouts ecstatically as Urban holds up a crucifix and tells his listeners to wear the cross as a symbol that "Christ died for you, and that it is your duty to die for him."

The response is passionate and immediate. Strips of red cloth appear as if from nowhere, and the crowd in the field begins fashioning them into crosses and sewing them onto garments. In the days that follow, some zealous followers will even brand their skin with crosses.

The battle cry has been sounded. The battle emblem has been forged. The engine of the Crusades—a mass movement unlike any other in history—has been set in motion. It will remain in motion for nearly two centuries.

The first Crusaders, however, are not the noblemen who stood in the field at Clermont. Instead, they are a mob of peasants and other poor people, incited by one Peter the Hermit, who may or may not be a monk, who walks barefoot, who lived for a time in Jerusalem, and who sustains himself on wine and fish. As charismatic in his way as the pope, Peter rallies his troops by simple force of conviction. They set out from Amiens, France, in March 1096, nearly 15,000 strong—men, women, and children, old and young, from as far away as Scotland, singing joyful hymns as they march.

It will be nearly half a year before the pope's army of knights and princes follows Peter's lead. By then Peter's "Poor People's Crusade" will have straggled across northern France and Rhineland, where, apparently eager to begin killing "infidels" even before they reach the Holy Land, they brutally slaughter thousands of Jews, whom they believe to be responsible for Christ's crucifixion. It is the first—and far from the last—in a series of anti-Semitic pogroms that will darken European history for centuries.

By the time Peter's followers reach Constantinople, the capital of the great Byzantine empire, they have disintegrated into a rabble, attacking villages, plundering, and murdering. Peter's crusade ends in utter disaster, with the peasants besieged in a Turkish fortress where they succumb to Turkish arrows and to starvation and thirst. Fewer than a third of their number survive. But Peter the Hermit and his legend endure. In

LEFT: One of many etchings from the Encyclopédie Médiévale, *by Eugène Viollet-le-Duc, used by the filmmakers as inspiration for costumes, weaponry, and set decoration.*

August 1096, the princes of Western Europe and their knightly battalions begin their own eastward march. Ambitious, well armed, and deeply committed to the cause, they will triumph where Peter and his followers have failed.

Cross and Crescent

To understand what has led to the First Crusade, it's necessary to go back several centuries, to the breakup in the third century C.E. of the old Roman Empire. The western half is overrun by successive waves of pagan invaders—Vandals, Ostrogoths, Franks, and Visigoths, among others—while the far more stable eastern half continues the traditions and style of imperial Rome overlain with the new Christian religion. This becomes known as the Byzantine empire. Its capital Byzantium, or Constantinople (present-day Istanbul), is named for its founder Constantine I, the first Christian emperor, who reigns in the fourth century C.E. Its citizens speak Greek and their religion becomes known as Greek Orthodoxy. To the west, the common language of the gradually Christianizing population is Latin and its religion Roman Catholic.

By the sixth century, the Franks—now the dominant tribe in Western Europe—have converted to Christianity. (In the late Roman Empire, the Franks were one of several Germanic tribes threatening Rome's Gallic provinces bordering the Rhine. Over several centuries they spread west and southward to establish a kingdom—first under Clovis and later Charlemagne—covering most of present-day France.) At the beginning of the seventh century, the Byzantine empire controls most of the Mediterranean, including Jerusalem and its surroundings. But sweeping changes are about to occur.

They arise out of a new religion, Islam, whose founder, Mohammed, dies in 632 C.E. His Muslim Arab followers begin an impressive advance into Northern Africa and Europe; they conquer Spain (which will remain Muslim-controlled for more than seven centuries) and Egypt, take over most of the Holy Land, and are defeated only when they reach France in 732. Their rule is mostly pacific, a golden age of science and the arts; Christians and Jews are tolerated, although they have second-class

ABOVE: *Concept art for Saladin's personal flag. It reads: "Glory to our Lord the Sultan, victorious king, father of conquest, Salah al Din Yusef ibn Ayyub, the warrior, reviver of the state, commander of the faithful."*

citizenship. Nevertheless, Arab ambition has not been completely quelled. Muslims see Byzantium as the gateway to Europe; if they can capture it, all Europe will be theirs.

Within the Holy Land itself, soon to become a religious battleground, a diverse population coexists: Jews, Muslims following both the Sunni and Shi'a traditions, and Christians of virtually every stripe—Greek Orthodox, Armenian, Maronite, Jacobite, and Nestorian. Although under Muslim rule, Jerusalem is largely Christian, and its principal shrine, the Church of the Holy Sepulchre—site of Jesus' burial—is untouched; Christian pilgrims are allowed to visit it unmolested.

The disruption begins in the middle of the eleventh century. The Seljuk Turks, nomadic herdsmen from Central Asia, conquer Persia and convert to Islam. Their conquests continue, now flavored by proselytizing zeal. They establish themselves in Baghdad in 1055 and begin sacking cities throughout the Middle East. Palestine, formerly under the control of the Egyptians, falls to the Seljuks in the early 1070s. With the Seljuk defeat of the Byzantine army in Armenia in 1071, the balance in the region shifts dramatically. For Christians living in the West, the implications are ominous: their pilgrimages to the Holy Land are now threatened.

It may be impossible for 21st-century people to grasp the significance of pilgrimage to medieval men and women. Shrines of all sorts were extremely meaningful, and those associated with Christ had the highest value. Pilgrimage provided an escape from everyday routine, a means of achieving redemption from sin, and—if the pilgrim was extremely fortunate or blessed—an occasion for a miraculous event. The desire for pilgrimage became an obsession as communications within Europe, and maritime traffic around the Mediterranean, improved.

By the late 11th and early 12th centuries C.E., the Seljuk Turks are proving vulnerable. Internal fighting among warlords and princes leads to the erosion of their empire, which in turn allows the Fatimid caliphs of Egypt to make inroads into their old dominions in the Holy Land.

It's a time of upheaval in the Christian West as well. In 1054 the Eastern and Western churches, at odds for centuries over doctrine and language, make a permanent split, known to historians as "the Great Schism." The pope in Rome places an anathema against the patriarch of Constantinople, who in turn excommunicates the pope and his followers.

LEFT: Ptolemais (Acre) given to Philip Augustus and Richard the Lionheart 13th July 1191, *by Merry Joseph Blondel, c. 1840s. The leaders of the Third Crusade took back the coastal city of Acre after a long and bitter siege.*

God has instituted in our time holy wars, so that the order of knights and the crowd running in its wake... might find a new way of gaining salvation. And so they are not forced to abandon secular affairs completely by choosing the monastic life or any religious profession, as used to be the custom, but can attain in some measure God's grace while pursuing their own careers, with the liberty and in the dress to which they are accustomed.

—GUIBERT OF NOGENT, ABBOT OF A MONASTERY IN NORTHEASTERN FRANCE, C. 1115

The theological split will prove lasting. Politically, however, the situation proves to be transitory.

Freed from ties to his eastern brethren, Pope Gregory VII, Urban II's predecessor, in 1073 orders sweeping changes within the Roman Catholic Church. His goal: to eliminate rampant immorality in the priesthood and to strengthen the papacy. Meanwhile, a crusading spirit has already captured the popular imagination in Spain and Sicily, where a form of "crusade" is already under way as western Christians battle to reclaim their former lands from Muslim control.

In 1081, Alexius Comnenus is crowned emperor of Byzantium. His empire is in disarray, and he is determined to restore it. For that, he realizes, he will need the help of his counterparts in the West. In 1093 he writes to Robert, Count of Flanders, a cousin of William the Conqueror, appealing "in the name of God" for military assistance. He details the persecution and humiliation of Greek Christians at the hands of the Turks and "Saracens"—a generic term for Muslim Arabs—and implores western princes to "act while there is still time lest the kingdom of the Christians shall vanish from your sight and, what is more important, the Holy Sepulchre shall vanish."

In case that appeal fails to entice his audience, he reminds them that the churches of Constantinople "are loaded with a vast treasure of gold and silver, gems and precious stones, mantles and cloths of silk," and that the city is home to "the most beautiful women in the Orient."

The letter finds its way to Pope Urban II, who is moved by its pious anguish, if not by its earthly allures. He sees his mission as unambiguous, sent directly from God.

The Rise of the Knight

For the most part, the knights who respond to Urban's call and prepare to engage in holy war are a far cry from the chivalric heroes later celebrated by poets and troubadours. Their very title, "knight," has lowly origins in *cnecht*, Old English for "boy," and *Knecht*, German for "servant." They have evolved from Roman foot soldiers into warriors mounted on horseback—a significant transformation that implies the wherewithal to buy, feed, and groom a horse and to pay for the armor and weaponry required for battle. For that reason, knights generally come from the ruling elites, and their distinctive appearance makes them a class apart.

They play an important role in the tumultuous culture of the early Middle Ages. It is a time characterized by rampant violence on every level of society. Governments lack the resources and communications to exert central authority, and rulers depend on alliances with knights and other elites to carry out their will.

But in the late 11th century the concept of chivalry is still nearly two centuries away. There is no system of heraldry to identify knightly clans, and no established dubbing rites: Any knight can make a knight out of another man, even a commoner, as Godfrey of Ibelin does with Balian in *Kingdom of Heaven*—and as the real Balian of Ibelin did with ordinary citizens during the siege of Jerusalem.

Yet the seeds of knightly tradition have already been planted. The early 11th century sees the institution of the "Truce of God," which forbids knights from attacking women and peasants and from waging battle on Sundays and holy days. From these early and limited strictures will evolve, by the late 13th century, an elaborate code of

I Dub Thee Knight

It's not certain how we got the popular image of a knight being newly invested by a tap on each shoulder with the flat of a sword. What's certain is that this was not part of any knighting ceremony used in the 12th century or even several centuries later. The sword was important to the ceremony, but was simply belted onto the new knight as a symbol of his rank. For the actual dubbing—as depicted in the scene where Godfrey knights Balian—the new knight received a hearty blow with an open hand from his sponsor.

A 12th-century source, *L'Ordene de chevalerie*, describes the procedure thus: "The candidate was first bathed, the bath symbolizing the washing away of his sins. Then he was clothed in a white robe symbolizing his determination to defend God's law.... In the church he was invested with his accoutrements: the gilded spur, to give him courage to serve God; the sword, to fight the enemy and 'protect the poor people from the rich.' Finally, he received the *colée*, a blow of the hand on the shoulder or head, 'in remembrance of Him who ordained you and dubbed you knight.'"

chivalry that requires knights to be brave, courageous, and physically superior to others; to right wrongs done to the defenseless; to never brandish a weapon in anger "or for evil purposes"; to fight fairly and honorably; and to defend the Church, the king, and the queen "unto death."

Many of the knights participating in the Crusades are under the command of noblemen who are brothers of princes and kings—men such as Robert, Duke of Normandy, brother of England's King William II; Hugh, Count of Vermandois, brother of the Frankish king Philip I; and Baldwin of Boulogne, younger son of Eustace II of Boulogne. Denied the throne themselves, these princes and barons seek glory, riches, and possibly new fiefdoms in "Outremer"—literally, "the land beyond the sea." Baldwin, in fact, will become the first king of the new Kingdom of Jerusalem.

Although Pope Urban's call is directed only at the wealthy elites, thousands of noncombatants—from illiterate peasants to intellectuals and tradespeople—also respond. Indeed, the Crusades exert a mass influence unequaled in history, before or since. Some Crusaders head east for religious reasons: to stand on holy ground, to retrace Jesus' steps, to be washed clean of sin. Some are part of the vast retinue of knights and princes: grooms, blacksmiths, cooks, armorers, foot soldiers, clerics, and even women. Other Crusaders are caught up in the spirit of adventure and novelty; to a medieval person unlikely to travel farther than 20 miles from his birthplace during his lifetime, the prospect of a thousand-mile journey seems thrillingly exotic. And still others are simply swept along by a communal momentum that exerts an exceptional pull in the Middle Ages, when the concept of individualism is barely formed.

The Princes' Crusade

Four contingents make up the army of the First Crusade: the northern French, the southern French, Germans and Lotharingians, and southern Italian Normans. Each group speaks a different language, has a different leader, and follows a different route. But by the time they reach the East, they are known collectively as "Franks." To this day, the Arabic word for "westerner" is "Franj."

In December 1096, two months after the Turks slaughtered Peter the Hermit's followers, the Princes' Crusade arrives at the gates of Constantinople. Alexius, despite the bitter lessons of the earlier crusade, provides food and supplies—and pledges even more—in return for promises that the Crusaders will cede any captured lands to him. Both sides affirm the promises. In due time, both sides will break them.

The grueling march across Asia Minor claims the lives of half the Crusaders and more than half of their horses. Many of the casualties occur during squabbles over captured booty; many others occur during the seven-month siege of Antioch, a great walled trading city—the richest on the Palestinian coast. The battle rages until June 28, 1098. In the end, the exhausted Crusaders kill almost everyone, including resident Greek, Syrian, and Armenian Christians.

Following this near-Pyrrhic victory, the surviving Crusader princes waste six months arguing amongst themselves about who would rule the captured city. In the end, the Count of Toulouse sets out for Jerusalem in January 1099, leaving behind his rival Bohemond, an ambitious and ruthless Norman prince who will take to calling himself the Prince of Antioch.

The march to the Holy City proves uneventful. But a very different situation awaits the Crusaders' arrival in June. The city's governor, Iftikhar ad-Daula, warned of the invaders' approach, has poisoned the wells around the city, brought flocks of goats and sheep inside the walls, and fortified the city's towers against bombardments with bales of cotton and hay. And he has summoned the Egyptian army for support.

But what is the office of the duly ordained soldiery? To defend the Church, to assail infidelity, to venerate the priesthood, to protect the poor from injuries, to pacify the province, to pour out their blood for their brothers (as the formula of their oath instructs them), and, if need be, to lay down their lives. The high priests of God are in their throat, and two-edged swords are in their hands to execute punishment on the nations and rebuke upon the peoples, and to bind their kings to chains and their nobles in links of iron. But to what end? To the end that they may serve madness, vanity, avarice, or their own private self-will? By no means. Rather to the end that they may execute the judgment that is committed to them to execute; wherein each follows not his own will but the deliberate decision of God, the angels, and men, in accordance with equity and the public utility.... For soldiers that do these things are "saints," and are the more loyal to their prince in proportion as they more zealously keep the faith of God; and they advance the more successfully the honour of their own valor as they seek the more faithfully in all things the glory but of their God.

—John of Salisbury, 12th century

"...on that day we fought with the strength given to us by God and conquered them, killing a great multitude. God was continually at our side and we returned with more than 200 heads, so that the people might rejoice at the sight of them...."

– Stephen, Count of Blois and Chartres, describing the siege of Antioch

The siege begins on June 7, but the Crusaders outside Jerusalem's walls, desperately short of water and wood, are as besieged as the defenders inside them. And, as usual, they are arguing among themselves–this time about the title of the future ruler of the city they intend to capture. Can the sovereign of Jerusalem properly be called "king," or does that title belong only to Christ?

On July 6, in the midst of the dissent and desperation, a priest named Peter Desiderius announces that he's had a vision: If the Crusaders walk barefoot around the walls of Jerusalem, in nine days the city will be theirs. Two days later, a remarkable procession takes place, led by priests and followed by knights–all barefoot–while the defending Saracens taunt and blaspheme from the parapets.

Now certain of victory, the Christians fight with renewed zeal. The Saracens hurl Greek fire (burning pitch and sulfur); the Christians fight back with flaming arrows that ignite the cotton and hay inside the towers. Their huge, mobile siege engines throw heavy rocks across the walls.

Finally, on July 15–the ninth day, exactly as Peter Desiderius has prophesied–Godfrey of Bouillon maneuvers a narrow bridge into position and leads an army of Crusaders in the walled city. They kill everyone in their path. Iftikhar, the governor, offers his treasure in exchange for his life and the life of his bodyguard. As a result, they are the only Saracens to escape the massacre.

It is a slaughter both deliberate and merciless that continues throughout the day and night. Men, women, and children alike are murdered; the invading army stampedes over the corpses. The city's terrified Jews seek refuge in the chief synagogue. The Crusaders set fire to it, with the Jews inside.

At the end of the long, bloody, and triumphant day, the Crusaders celebrate Mass at the Church of the Holy Sepulchre. The Kingdom of Jerusalem is securely in Christian hands–for now.

The Kingdom of Jerusalem

The first ruler of Jerusalem, Godfrey of Bouillon, piously refuses the title of king, preferring "Advocate of the Holy Sepulchre." Those who come after him as rulers are not so scrupulous. Godfrey's younger brother, Baldwin, who succeeds him, is crowned by no lesser personage than the

OVERLEAF: Taking of Jerusalem by the Crusaders, 15th July 1099, *by Emile Signol, 1847. In this fanciful imagining, the mounted Godfrey of Bouillon gives thanks to God. At left is Peter the Hermit, who actually died earlier and far from Jerusalem.*

papal legate, the archbishop of Pisa. Baldwin wears a mantle on his shoulders and loves the trappings of monarchy.

Under Baldwin's rule, the Franks expand their kingdom, conquering Acre (present-day Akko) and Tortosa and establishing dominion over the other Crusader states in the north. By the time of his death in 1118, Baldwin I's empire stretches from the County of Edessa in northern Syria all the way to the Red Sea, a patchwork of territories studded with Crusader castles.

The emir who commanded the tower of David surrendered to the Count [of St. Gilles] and opened the gate where pilgrims used to pay tribute. Entering the city, our pilgrims pursued and killed the Saracens up to the temple of Solomon. There the Saracens assembled and resisted fiercely all day, so that the whole temple flowed with their blood. At last the pagans were overcome and our men seized many men and women in the temple, killing them or keeping them alive as they saw fit. On the roof of the temple there was a great crowd of pagans of both sexes, to whom Tancred and Gaston de Beert gave their banners [to provide them with protection]. Then the crusaders scattered throughout the city, seizing gold and silver, horses and mules, and houses full of all sorts of goods. Afterwards our men went rejoicing and weeping for joy to adore the sepulchre of our Saviour Jesus and there discharged their debt to Him....

– Anonymous Christian eyewitness, account published before 1101

Over the next half century a succession of rulers—some brilliant, some feckless—assume the throne. But it can be argued that the real rulers of the kingdom are the knightly orders that have gained power since the conquest of Jerusalem. Like monastic orders, they subject their members to a highly regulated life that includes charitable acts; unlike monks, the knights combine religion with fighting. The Knights Templar, founded in Jerusalem around 1120, is the earliest of these orders. It takes its name from the building the Crusaders believe to be Solomon's Temple (in fact destroyed in 586 B.C.E.), where it has its headquarters. Its primary function is to provide protection to Christian pilgrims. The other principal military order is the Knights Hospitaler, originally a brotherhood that cared for the poor and sick at the Hospital of St. John; by the mid-1130s, it has added military duties to its function. Both of these orders owe their allegiance to the pope, not the king; they will in time become extremely wealthy landowners.

Baldwin I dies without heirs and is succeeded by his cousin, Baldwin II, who continues the kingdom's expansion. But his son, Baldwin III, is still a boy when he assumes the throne. Recognizing potential weakness, the Muslim ruler of Mosul (in present-day Iraq), captures Edessa. Over the protests of the kingdom's nobility, the kings of far-off France and Germany seize the opportunity to attack Damascus, a doomed adventure known as the Second Crusade.

Baldwin III, the first king of Jerusalem to have been born in Outremer, is also the first representative of a new "orientalized" generation of Franks. He cements relations with Constantinople by marrying a 13-year-old Byzantine princess and by hosting the Byzantine emperor on a tour of the Holy

The Lure of the Orient

As new generations were born in the Kingdom of Jerusalem, they gradually lost their western identity. Many learned to speak Greek, Arabic, and other eastern languages; some intermarried with Greeks or Armenians—even with Muslims. They grew accustomed to the warm climate and languid, sumptuous lifestyle of their adopted homeland, and reveled in their new status and wealth. As the crusading historian Fulcher of Chartres observed shortly before the death of Baldwin II, "Those who were poor in the West, God has made rich in the East. Those who had little money there have innumerable bezants here, and a man who did not even have a house in the West now possesses a city. Why return to the West when there is an Orient like this?"

Most Crusaders, of course, did return to the West, bringing with them ideas from the East. Prior to the Crusades, for example, European castles had been small and made of wood; after exposure to Arab architecture, they became massive stone structures. Scientific and medical concepts also filtered westward, as well as literary ones. The songs of the Provençal troubadors, with their themes of courtly love, owe much to Arab poetry introduced by returning Crusaders.

Land. His death is mourned by Christian and Muslim subjects alike.

Baldwin III is succeeded by his younger brother Amalric, who leads his army into Egypt against the great Turkish general Nur-ad-Din. He is the first king of Jerusalem to journey to Cairo, and his activities there are not only military. In a historic encounter, Amalric's emissary, Hugh of Caesarea, meets with the 16-year-old caliph—who has the status of a demideity—and clasps bare hands with him.

The Egyptian adventure is also the setting for another significant encounter. It is here that the Crusader army, in alliance with the Egyptian vizier, Shawar, engages with a young and promising Turkish commander named Saladin. Saladin is forced to retreat to Damascus in disappointment. But within a year and a half he will return to Cairo in triumph.

Saladin and the Leper King

Salah al-Din Yusuf Ibn Ayyub, known to Western history as Saladin, is born into a Kurdish clan in Tikrit (now Iraq) in 1137. He is educated in Damascus, which has recently become a center of Islamic orthodoxy. Mosques and madrassas—religious schools—have begun preaching the doctrine of *jihad*, or holy war in the name of Allah. Saladin is an avid pupil, but his early career is devoted to fighting Muslims rather than Christians—in Aleppo, in Masyaf, and in Mosul. By 1169 he is master of Egypt; in 1174 he takes Damascus. After several failed attempts, he finally takes Aleppo, in June 1183. His next mission, he promises, will be the conquest of Jerusalem—home of two of the greatest shrines in Islam and the ultimate prize of *jihad*.

"I think that when God grants me victory over the rest of Palestine, I shall divide my territories, make a will stating my wishes, then set sail on this sea for their far-off lands and pursue the Franks there, so as to free the earth from anyone who does not believe in Allah, or die in the attempt."

– SALADIN TO HIS FRIEND BAHA AD-DIN

And his ambitions do not stop there. He tells his friend Baha ad-Din: "I think that when God grants me victory over the rest of Palestine, I shall divide my territories, make a will stating my wishes, then set sail on this sea for their far-off lands and pursue the Franks there, so as to free the earth from anyone who does not believe in Allah, or die in the attempt."

The Crusaders have met their match: a man as fervently religious as they, and equally as unwavering in his determination to use violence to achieve his ends. His enemies, Muslim and Christian, see him as an ambitious adventurer. Curiously, though, later generations in West and East will view him with great admiration. "Saladin was... a man of humble enough birth, but of great and loftiest spirit and highly trained in deeds of war," writes the 14th-century Italian novelist Boccaccio. "He was munificent in giving and of his magnificence one cannot say enough."

In 1174, Saladin's mentor and rival Nur ad-Din dies suddenly in Damascus. The same year, the Frankish king Amalric dies in Jerusalem. (Amalric's widow, Maria Comnena, marries the historical Balian of Ibelin, an established lord of Outremer and not the humble French artisan of the screenplay.) Amalric's successor is his young son, Baldwin IV, one of the most sympathetic and tragic heroes in Crusades history.

When Baldwin is ten, his tutor, William of Tyre, makes a disturbing discovery: the boy can endure pain longer than any of his friends. Consulting the writings of the ancient Greek physician Hippocrates, William correctly diagnoses the reasons for Baldwin's preternatural fortitude. He has leprosy. Doctors–among them a Muslim–are consulted, but the disease progresses inexorably, gradually attacking Baldwin's face and limbs. Yet although his condition is well known, no one in court speaks publicly of it.

Baldwin is just 13 when he takes the throne; until he comes of age, he is assigned a guardian, Raymond of Tripoli ("Tiberias" in the film), a man of great reason and courage regarded by his Arab counterparts as "the ablest Crusader of his time." After Baldwin comes of age, because of worries about his health, a regent is appointed. This man, Reynald of Chatillon, is in many ways Raymond's opposite: greedy, reckless, and selfish. He has already spent 16 years in an Aleppo jail as Nur

RIGHT: Detail of Battle between Crusaders and Moslems, *artist unknown, 14th century. The Saracen's curved blade was a popular image, but most Saracen swords of the film's period were straight-edged.*

ad-Din's prisoner, during which time no one in the Kingdom of Jerusalem could be troubled to pay his ransom.

Yet for all his virtues, it is Raymond who unwittingly will contribute most to the downfall of the kingdom. Just before Baldwin IV's ascension to the throne, Raymond makes an enemy of a powerful Flemish knight, Gerard of Ridfort, by reneging on a promise of betrothal to a suitable wife. Gerard swears vengeance—and he will have it, at the expense of the Crusader dominion.

It is also Raymond who, in 1177, precipitates the first encounter between Saladin and the Franks in the Holy Land. When Raymond takes a large contingent of the king's army to fight in the north, Saladin seizes the opportunity to attack from the south. Baldwin has been left with a remnant of no more than 375 troops; Saladin commands 26,000 light-armed cavalry, 8,000 men on camels, and 1,000 bodyguards. Yet Baldwin's army manages to occupy the southern port of Ascalon just a few hours before Saladin reaches it. Instead of attacking, Saladin continues on to Jerusalem, burning and slaughtering along the way. Baldwin's tiny force ambushes the much larger Saracen army, which Saladin has optimistically left unguarded; 17-year-old Baldwin, visibly wasted by disease, fights in the vanguard. A sudden cold snap and heavy thunderstorms decimate the remainder of Saladin's men.

Over the next three years, a series of battles exhaust both sides. In 1180, Saladin and Baldwin sign a truce. It lasts less than a year, its rupture brought about by the ever-venal Reynald of Chatillon, who—not satisfied with his wife's vast landholdings, from Hebron to the Red Sea—decides to invade Arabia and destroy Muslim holy sites. Adding grave insult to injury, he also attacks a caravan that happens to be carrying Saladin's sister (or aunt; historians disagree). The story line of *Kingdom of Heaven* closely parallels these events.

Saladin prepares his revenge with care. After taking Aleppo in 1183 and becoming the most powerful man in Islam, he marches out of Damascus, determined to drive the Christians into the sea.

In his first encounter with them, at the Plains of Esdraelon, the Franks are led by Guy of Lusignan, a handsome, courtly, and ignorant man who is married to Baldwin's sister Sibylla. The battle ends without a victor, and Saladin decides to focus his hostilities against Reynald of Chatillon, who has barricaded himself in his castle, Kerak of Moab. Saladin attacks the castle for two months without success and finally retreats, only to return the following summer. This time, Baldwin, dying, is carried into battle on a litter. Once again Saladin is forced to retreat, and Baldwin enters the castle victorious.

It is Baldwin's last triumph. He dies in March 1185, at 24, his face, hands, and feet eaten away by leprosy. He is revered by Christians and admired by Muslims. "The leper child knew how to make his authority respected," writes Saladin's secretary, Imad ad-Din of Isfahan.

The Fall of Jerusalem

Toward the end of his life, Baldwin had been determined that his brother-in-law, the inept and potentially dangerous Guy of Lusignan, not inherit the throne. Instead, his five-year-old nephew is crowned Baldwin V in the Church of the Holy Sepulchre; Raymond of Tripoli is his regent. A skilled diplomat, Raymond negotiates a

The devil and his crew were taken, the King and his counts were captured, and the Sultan sat down to review his chief prisoners, who came forward stumbling in their fetters like drunken men. The Grand Master of the Templars was brought in in his sins, and many of the Templars and Hospitalers with him. The King Guy and his brother Geoffrey were escorted in, with Hugh of Jubail, Humphrey, and Prince Arnat of al-Karak [as the Muslims called Reynald of Chatillon], who was the first to fall into the net. The Sultan had vowed to have his blood and had said: "When I find him I shall kill him immediately."

— Imad ad-Din, reporting on the aftermath of the Battle of Hattin

four-year truce with Saladin. The boy king is sickly, however, and in August 1186 he dies—possibly of natural causes, possibly from poison. Over the protests of the barons of the kingdoms, the boy's mother, Sibylla, is crowned queen. She immediately removes the crown from her head and places it on the head of her husband, Guy.

Guy's utter incompetence is not lost on Saladin, who wastes no time building up his forces in violation of the truce. Meanwhile, Reynald of Chatillon chooses this ill-timed moment in early 1187 for another act of brigandry and provocation, ambushing a large caravan en route from Cairo to Damascus and imprisoning all of its Muslim travelers. King Guy intercedes, but to no avail: Reynald considers himself beyond the law of Jerusalem.

Saladin has had enough; he is ready for *jihad* in earnest. His strategy is to march along the shores of the Sea of Galilee, take the city of Tiberias, and continue south to Jerusalem. Raymond of Tripoli urges King Guy to sacrifice Tiberias: There aren't enough springs between Jerusalem and Tiberias, he argues convincingly, to water the king's army. Guy and the barons nod in agreement. But then Gerard of Ridfort, Raymond's sworn enemy, gets the king's ear. "Raymond is betraying you, sire," he hisses. "Take up battle formations and follow the banner of the Holy Cross!"

And so, in the scorching dawn of July 3, 1187, Guy's army marches to the Sea of Galilee. Tiberias is already in flames; as Raymond has warned, water is in desperately short supply. The army camps in the crater of an extinct volcano between two hills known as the Horns of Hattin, impossible terrain for heavily armed horsemen. And it gets worse: Saladin's men set fire to the dry grass, creating huge clouds of thick smoke. At dawn, the Muslim archers attack a Christian army already half-dead from thirst and suffocating in heavy armor. The battle continues through the next day, when at last the surviving Christians lie on the ground too exhausted to surrender. Among the most devastating of their losses is the True Cross, which had been carried into battle by a bishop who was captured. Its fate remains a mystery.

Saladin takes an illustrious group of prisoners, among them King Guy, Balian of Ibelin, and Reynald of Chatillon. He spares the first two, but personally stabs Reynald to death and mounts his head on a lance. The message is unmistakable: Saladin has broken the back of the Kingdom of Jerusalem. All that remains to be conquered is the Holy City itself.

One captive is paroled and allowed to return to

Jerusalem. This is Balian of Ibelin, who asks to look after his ailing wife, Maria Comnena, the widow of Amalric I. Saladin, a great believer in the divine protection of kings—even Christian kings—grants this request.

Balian arrives in Jerusalem to find chaos. As the highest-ranking surviving officer, he places himself in charge and prepares for siege. He makes every boy of noble descent a knight, takes possession of the treasury, and brings in corn from neighboring villages to sustain the population.

Meanwhile, Saladin quickly captures the coastal cities of Jaffa, Acre, Haifa, Caesarea, and Ascalon. In Ascalon on September 4, during a partial eclipse of the sun, he meets with a delegation from Jerusalem and offers surrender terms. They are angrily refused.

In response, Saladin advances his siege engines on the walled city of Jerusalem. Balian's men surge out of the walls and destroy them. The Christians' situation is desperate, but they are prepared for martyrdom.

Finally, on September 30, Balian comes to Saladin's tent to sue for terms. If they are not met, he warns, he and his followers will set fire to Jerusalem and destroy all the holy places. Saladin, alarmed by Balian's zeal, agrees to treat the city's population as prisoners, and sets ransom amounts: ten gold pieces for each man, five for each woman, and one for each child.

The downfall comes quickly and surprisingly peacefully, on September 30, 1187—especially when compared to the Crusaders' bloody conquest 88 years earlier. There are no murders, no rapes, no looting—not by Muslims, anyway. Saladin releases all the old people without requiring a ransom. When Heraclius, the Christian patriarch of Jerusalem, is seen leaving with city with gold plate from the churches, Saladin allows him to pass unharmed. Saladin's brother takes a thousand poor people as slaves, and then releases them all. Saladin himself is said to weep when he sees the tears of Christian women. And after three days, he opens the Church of the Holy Sepulchre to Christian pilgrims.

It is not quite the final curtain. There will be two more Crusades to avenge the losses. Richard Lionheart will campaign with some success in Palestine, and Constantinople will be sacked by Crusaders. But the fall of Jerusalem to Saladin marks the real and symbolic end of Outremer—the end of the Latin kingdom of the East.

Right: Orlando Bloom as Balian defends the walls of Jerusalem.

By the virtue and power of God we have taken possession of Jerusalem and its territories; and of the three cities that still remain in the hands of the Christians: Tyre, Tripoli, and Antioch, nothing remains but that we shall occupy them also. But if you desire war, we shall meet you with the power of God, who wills of his good pleasure that we shall occupy the whole land of the Christians. If you want peace, you have only to command the captains of these three cities to deliver them up to us, and we shall restore to you the Holy Cross, and we shall liberate the Christian captives in all our territory, and we will be at peace with you.

— From a letter written by Saladin to the German Emperor Frederick I Barbarossa, shortly after the fall of Jerusalem

Dramatizing the Crusades

The creative engine that Ridley Scott and writer William Monahan ignited to work on *Tripoli* barely paused when that film was postponed. It just shifted gears and started rolling down the road toward *Kingdom of Heaven*. Between the November 2001 meeting where the film was conceived and when shooting wrapped in Morocco in June 2004, a remarkable collaboration unfolded over the writing, development, and shooting of the film story—a process Monahan recalls as a sustained high point of his working life.

"The minute Ridley said 'Crusades' I knew it was going to be the fall of the Latin Kingdom of Jerusalem to Saladin. It would have been absolutely the same had he asked me on September 10th. But as a matter of general interest, we met not long after the World Trade Center attack. You could still smell the fire, the toxicity in the air, in Manhattan. The two civilizations, arguably, being again at war, I was interested in examining a time when there was a period of... if not peace, then accommodation—when the Muslim world and 'Christendom' were at an equal strength.

"Baldwin IV, the idea of him in a silver mask, had haunted me since I was fourteen or so. Not precisely the historical Baldwin but the idea of what could be done with him in a drama or a book. You hang onto all sorts of ideas and impressions as an artist, and often you never get a chance to use them. They're in storage, perfectly good, but nobody's asking.

"But then someone does, and of all things, it's Ridley Scott. It was an amazing opportunity to write this work under his protection. He cultivated me and I cultivated the story, and then we pitched in together to refine it and get it through the studio process and onto the screen."

Because the *Tripoli* script had demonstrated that Monahan could write historical drama for film, he was left more or less alone to draft

Left: Pikemen and flag-bearers in the Army of Jerusalem.

Kingdom of Heaven. "Ridley got engaged full bore after the draft was written," Monahan notes. "At that point anyone can say anything, and I welcome it, but writing the 'working text' is a solitary operation. You need a work that could be filmed. Then you dig into it with the director and make the one that will be."

The writer had his characters for *Kingdom of Heaven* from the get-go: Baldwin, Sibylla, Reynald of Chatillon, among others. "And then, of course, if you pick the Latin Kingdom of Jerusalem as your period, your hero has to be Balian of Ibelin, and your natural fifth act is his defense of Jerusalem against Saladin. I've always been fascinated by Saladin, as the chivalrous figure every contemporary observer found him to be."

Monahan was also fascinated—as was Scott—by the way that the Europeans living in Jerusalem had become "orientalized," to an extent that the pope execrated them as "you silken, luxurious lords of Outremer." Noting that the Crusade had collapsed into accommodation, except for the actions of fanatics like Reynald, he says "I was interested in the accommodation, the commingling of cultures. It's cinematically compelling on every level, including the design standpoint."

Monahan was familiar with most of the primary historical documents, but he went back and read everything to make sure that there wasn't a better story to be extracted from the material. There was not, he concluded.

The minute Ridley said "Crusades" I knew it was going to be the fall of the Latin Kingdom of Jerusalem to Saladin... I was interested in examining a time when the Muslim world and "Christendom" were at an equal strength.

– Screenwriter William Monahan

Doing the Research

In researching the history, he used chiefly primary sources—for example, the accounts of William of Tyre (c. 1130–1185), regarded by historians as among the greatest chroniclers of any age. Born in Syria to French parents, he became archbishop of Tyre and chancellor to the Kingdom of Jerusalem, as well as the personal tutor of Baldwin IV. William's writings show an acute awareness of the strengths and failings of both warring cultures. "I also used the Lyon Eracles (an anonymous French chronicler), and a lot of Muslim writers such as Imad ad-Din and Usama Ibin Munquidh, for incident, color, and perspective," says Monahan, who found the primary

Right: King Guy's army marches out of Jerusalem, carrying with them the purported True Cross, to meet their doom at the Battle of Hattin.

materials perfectly accessible and far more interesting than the histories made out of them. "When I'm doing history I'm interested in my own take and am very scrupulous about going to the primary sources."

Monahan had a pretty good library to begin with, and Scott's production company made sure he had any books he needed—including some hard-to-find volumes. "For a creative writer doing history, the technique is to read everything and then use what you need—which often is very little. But you need to read everything. I have the sort of brain that assays stuff on the spot for dramatic usefulness, and I get scenes sort of alchemically while reading. It's all there in the writer, anyway; if there's nothing for the original material to resonate with, nothing happens."

The value of historical fiction always lies apart from its historicity, Monahan feels. "A writer worth his salt is always going to make a subject his own, consider his own take the vital one. That's not a deficiency but a necessity." Shakespeare's *Henry V*, he points out, is not history but drama. "No one should expect stage plays or screenplays to be history. And historiography is never 'historically accurate.' All historians of this period use the same handful of texts, most of which are terrifically entertaining but prejudiced and unreliable—not only toward the Muslim or Christian sides but from author to author."

In writing for film, he continues, one has to make assumptions and balance one text against another, just as a historian does. "In our case I think we have tried to do something very balanced and ethical."

Turning History into Story

Monahan's chosen time frame in the Crusades yielded incidents and characters of great richness and complexity, which became grist for his dramatic mill. He didn't feel at all distanced by the 1,000 years between them and us; in some ways found it an advantage. "Once you get out of the din and glare of the present, you can think properly about what's universal about human beings, human motives. The dramatist's job is to represent the universal facts of human experience, to raise a mirror to nature."

Characters in historical fiction typically are a mixture of "real" personages, with details of their lives altered or embroidered, and

invented characters whose point of view gives the reader or viewer a window on the period and its people, or fills in puzzling omissions in the historical record. Balian, on whom the plot hinged, needed a largely fictional treatment; the real Balian was an established lord of Outremer, not a French artisan. There are key places where the tracks of the real Balian and the film Balian converge, especially near the end. For example, "the original Balian volunteered to make the impossible defense of Jerusalem because he was begged to do so by the people," says Monahan. But this had a different prelude in history than in the film. "Balian actually was captured at the battle of Hattin and had to go to Saladin and ask his permission to return to Jerusalem. Saladin granted that permission. That tells you a lot about Balian, and even more about Saladin."

Among the featured characters, the only wholly invented ones are Godfrey of Ibelin (Liam Neeson) and the Hospitaler (David Thewlis). Godfrey would be fairly typical of a younger son of a lord, who went to the Holy Land to make his fortune. He is also, says Monahan, "the Crusader who has learned tolerance through experience. In the original draft he had what we called the 'pope scene,' in which he takes on the pope in Rome." The Hospitaler was created to show Christianity "done right," as the writer puts it, and to balance the more hot-headed, fanatical Christians in the story. "He expresses the way I feel about religion: Do the right thing and don't worry about the rest of it."

Certain characters and their behavior were deliberately tweaked for story purposes, while remaining relatively faithful to historical models. "Reynald of Chatillon is cooled a bit as a prime instigator of the catastrophe," notes Monahan, "because it was thought that Guy de Lusignan should be more of an autonomous villain rather than the confused and easily led man described by his contemporaries." The princess Sibylla, according to most histories, was actually devoted to Guy, choosing him over more worthy suitors put forth by the king after her first husband died. The film story needed a stronger and wiser Sibylla. But as Monahan notes, looking into the hearts of historical figures is tricky. Maybe Sibylla loved Guy, maybe not. "And that 'maybe not' makes good drama," says the writer.

Left: Concept drawing of the battle for Jerusalem, by Pier Luigi Basile.

In both writing and reading history, he advises, one should beware of any depiction—whether advertised as fiction or history—that suggests human beings were less complicated than we are today. Common sense should be exercised. Monahan takes issue with historians who maintain that Crusaders went to the Holy Land only for religious reasons. "Before 1492 the Holy Land was the only real outlet for ambition, the only theater of advancement for landless men. And I think it's problematic to interpret the European Middle Ages as an age of faith in which everyone believed the same thing. There were doubters, disbelievers, hypocrites, opportunists, and practical worldly men, as there are in any age.

"You have to avoid clichés and you have to avoid using people to advance a thesis. You're not doing a thesis. You're doing a picture of life in a world that has the same laws of gravity and attraction, and the same ordinary human needs and behavior as our own."

From Draft to Shooting Script

Once Monahan had finished his first draft, the script went through a series of revisions—which didn't really end, of course, until the last scene had been shot. The principal collaborator was always Ridley Scott, through Lisa Ellzey at Scott Free, and production executives at Fox were closely involved.

Scott had said at the outset that he didn't want a "palace drama with aristocrats swanning around the place," but Monahan was committed to his philosopher-king in a silver mask, "and you're going to have a few scenes in the throne room." He came in with a script that justified the track he was taking. In terms of historical fidelity, "it's safe to say that the script was more accurate before we made changes and cuts—but only in that it was longer, included more peripheral incident and personalities, and hadn't been subjected to the process of making it into a budgetable film—a process which was editorial."

That the first script was very long was intentional: Monahan

Ridley has an amazing capacity to keep the whole project in his head, from story to design to any element you can mention.

— William Monahan

* ATOM ☆ BOMB (13)
DESERT — AFTERMATH.
(ROAD · TO · DAMASCUS)
REYNALD SURVEYS.
DESTRUCTION ---"
(SALADINS SISTER.) "I AM"
REYNALD — "I · KNOW"

WAR: ROOM (18) ★
GUY TRYING TO BE
LEADER -- TILL -- BALIAN
ADDRESSES THE ROOM.
WITH A LOGICAL PLAN.
GUY ENRAGED AT ADVICE
IS BLIND TO LOGIC.

Above: Ridley Scott's 3 x 5 beat cards help him track key points in the film story. Opposite: Scott with screenwriter William Monahan on the Jerusalem set.

wanted to give Scott a lot to choose from. One climactic event in the story now takes place offstage, a decision that both trimmed the budget and avoided having a second great battle scene seem anticlimactic. "The battle of Hattin was removed," notes Monahan, "because as I had written it it would have cost a lot of money, and we didn't need it. We did not, dramatically, need Balian to go off with the Army of Jerusalem. (Both Balian and Tiberias, aka Raymond of Tripoli, actually fought with King Guy's army at Hattin.) We needed to apply the money elsewhere, and we didn't need a huge battle scene, considering that we are heading towards the epic defense of Jerusalem. So out it came. Instead we focused on the aftermath of the battle and Saladin's execution of Reynald—which in truth is all we needed dramatically."

The first stage of revision was trimming length to arrive at the version Fox greenlighted. Then Monahan and Scott got down to work scene by scene, virtually word by word. At one point during development, Monahan joined Scott on the West Coast to work intensively on the script for more than a month. Workdays averaged nine hours a day, seven days a week. Says Scott Free's Lisa Ellzey, "Ridley likes to read through the entire script out loud and do what he calls a 'running order.' He writes out each scene on a 3-by-5 card, then forcefully punches it into a bulletin board. We move the cards around, looking at where the characters are, where the action is."

Monahan adds, "It's extraordinary to be in a room with Ridley, working on a film of this scope. His artistry is profound: he's the best at what he does, and when he detects talent in others he'll do anything to advance it."

Scott also makes extensive notes in longhand, sometimes page after page, and fills the margins of his scripts with annotations and "Ridleygrams"—his famous off-the-cuff sketches. "Ridley will draw while thinking," says Monahan. "He has an amazing capacity to keep the whole project in his head, from story to design to any other element you can mention, and at any moment he can 'tell' you the story

74.

CONTINUED:

REYNALD
Sometimes they are chivalrous. They learned it from us.

INT. THE COURTYARD AT KERAK. MOMENTS LATER

BALIAN and his men stagger in, acclaimed by the peasants they have saved. Through the crowd comes Reynald.

REYNALD
You've given me more mouths to feed and more shit to throw over the wall. You have a great deal to learn about sieges.

BALIAN doesn't respond. REYNALD claps him on the arm.

REYNALD (CONT'D)
(whispering)
But that was magnificent.

BALIAN, looking up, sees SIBYLLA. She stands in an archway. Smiling down.

INT. A BEDCHAMBER AT KERAK. DAY

BALIAN looks at SIBYLLA in the gloom. We hear the preparations for battle going on. Cries in the night.

SIBYLLA
I see a man who will be great, unless he prefers to be good.

BALIAN
You wish your husband dead.

SIBYLLA takes it well. Philosophical.

SIBYLLA
If he is dead I have one course. If he is alive...I have another.
(looks up at Balian)
I will not lose Jerusalem. My grandfather took it in blood. I will keep it the same way, or any way I can.

BALIAN
We may not survive this siege.

SIBYLLA
No one kills princesses. It's somewhere written down.

(CONTINUED)

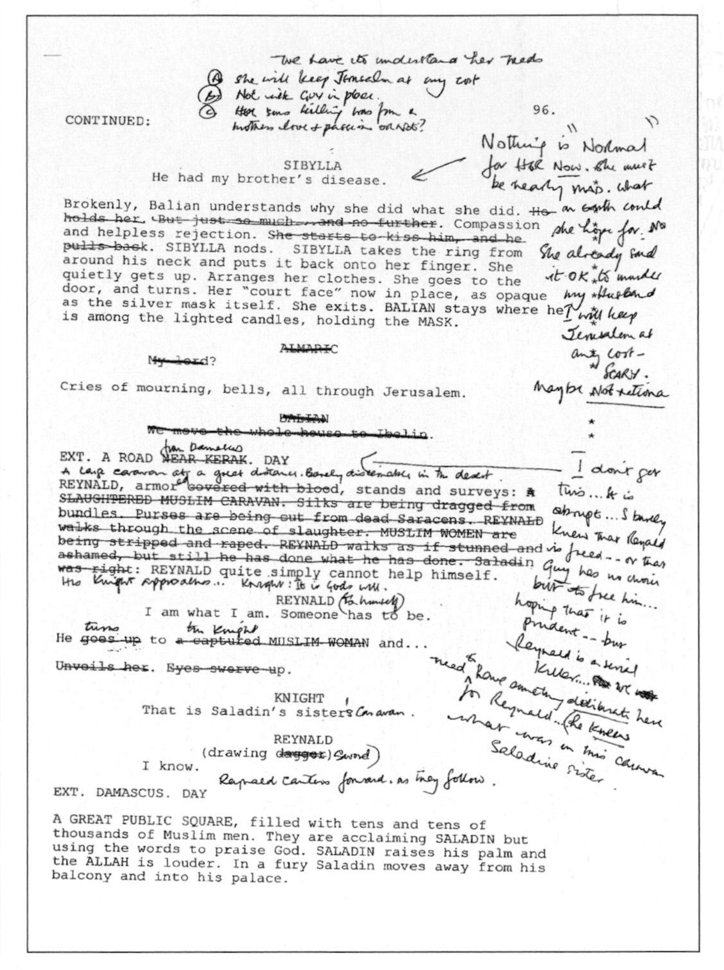

96.

CONTINUED:

SIBYLLA
He had my brother's disease.

Brokenly, Balian understands why she did what she did. He holds her. But just so much... and no further. Compassion and helpless rejection. She starts to kiss him, and he pulls back. SIBYLLA nods. SIBYLLA takes the ring from around his neck and puts it back onto her finger. She quietly gets up. Arranges her clothes. She goes to the door, and turns. Her "court face" now in place, as opaque as the silver mask itself. She exits. BALIAN stays where he is among the lighted candles, holding the MASK.

ALMARIC
My lord?

Cries of mourning, bells, all through Jerusalem.

BALIAN
We move the whole house to Ibelin.

EXT. A ROAD NEAR KERAK. DAY

REYNALD, armor covered with blood, stands and surveys: a SLAUGHTERED MUSLIM CARAVAN. Silks are being dragged from bundles. Purses are being cut from dead Saracens. REYNALD walks through the scene of slaughter. MUSLIM WOMEN are being stripped and raped. REYNALD walks as if stunned and ashamed, but still he has done what he has done. Saladin was right: REYNALD quite simply cannot help himself.

REYNALD
I am what I am. Someone has to be.

He goes up to a captured MUSLIM WOMAN and...

Unveils her. Eyes swerve up.

KNIGHT
That is Saladin's sister.

REYNALD
(drawing dagger)
I know.

EXT. DAMASCUS. DAY

A GREAT PUBLIC SQUARE, filled with tens and tens of thousands of Muslim men. They are acclaiming SALADIN but using the words to praise God. SALADIN raises his palm and the ALLAH is louder. In a fury Saladin moves away from his balcony and into his palace.

chronologically, which I can't do. I just have a grasp of the whole in sort of a brusque idiot-savant way. I know a thing is in key or it isn't but can't tell you why."

Scott is always probing the storyline for inspired moments, glints of light, telling details that bring the movie to life. Some involve major shifts in the screenplay (see sidebar), others are small insights that coalesce into a complete picture. Scott, for example, envisioned that Balian's wife would plant a tree early in the film (in flashback), and near the end Balian would revisit the tree, now grown larger and full of buds. Also in the European opening, he came up with a motto that Balian's blacksmith "father" had carved into a beam in his forge, and

Above: Scott's annotated pages from the script. (Note: These early pages do not correspond to the final cut of the film seen in theaters.) Right: Godfrey of Ibelin's party of Crusaders traveling through France. The mounted figures are the Hospitaler (David Thewlis), Firuz (Eriq Ebouaney), and the English Sergeant (Kevin McKidd).

A French Connection

Ridley Scott, says Monahan, made one master stroke during script development that changed the course of the film, opening it up both dramatically and visually: "I was hesitant at first about bringing Balian down from France–I initially started with the shipwreck, which we still have in the film: I had an image of all of medieval European civilization strewn across a beach as the opening, followed by the apparition of a fantastical Saracen knight. But Ridley insisted, brilliantly, that I try a French opening and not bother about time compression, which was weighing on my mind at first.

"So I went off and invented the French opening, and was literally transported by the act of doing so. That's where the movie stopped being just good and became very good indeed. I think it's a well-made opening to a drama. By having Balian arrive in the Kingdom of Jerusalem after his long journey, we are all discovering everything about this world together. It's very effective dramatically."

which Balian later shows to Godfrey: "What man is a man who does not make the world better?" Another detail came from Scott's life: he gave Sibylla's son a toy figurine of a knight to play with during his first meeting with Balian—a figure much like one Scott himself once owned.

Ellzey recalls how, during one script session, Scott mused about how the knights, trekking through the rain in France, might have kept their chainmail from rusting: by rubbing animal fat into the links. Just before the forest ambush scene, the character called the English Sergeant is seen in the background doing precisely that.

"Ridley is a fiend about details," she avers. "He had to know how much something would have weighed, how long it was, how much

Below: Balian and Godfrey practice swordsmanship while the English Sergeant (far right) oils his armor.

medieval coin it would have cost." Such details are critical to Scott's story process and give his imagined worlds great authority.

Particpating in story decisions throughout development were Tom Rothman and Jim Gianopulos, co-chairmen of Fox Filmed Entertainment; Hutch Parker; and the supervising executive on the project, Steve Asbell. All have enormous respect for Scott and his creative collaborators, while also recognizing that directors and writers need outside feedback when deeply immersed in story details.

The film proposes that it's better to live together than to be at war. That reason is better than fanaticism. If that gets across, then I did my job.

– William Monahan

The final shooting script remained close to Monahan's original conception in its overall story arc and character set, and the writer is philosophical about the tug of war in which screenwriters, directors, and studios inevitably engage. "This is a business in which individual work has to proceed under many expert eyes. In film, even though your first thought about a scene often turns out to be the right one, you can't insist on your first thought. It's a process of discovery. Typically with this script we would end up at a third position that was better than either the first thought or the counterproposal. That's exciting and perhaps not usual."

Writing on Location

Once principal photography got underway, Monahan accompanied the production to all the primary locations, to be available for on-the-spot rewrites and consulting with the cast and crew. In Spain and Morocco, he spent most of his time doing revisions well ahead of what was being shot—"doing little bits or micro-changes almost every day"—but mainly he was planning out the awesome siege of Jerusalem, months before those scenes were due to be shot in Ouarzazate.

Monahan absorbed an important lesson about his craft from this experience. "There are times when you realize you need a script change only when you're looking at the actual physical locations." And he was grateful for the opportunity to stay involved as the script evolved. "This stuff is usually vamped without input from writers, and that's one of the million ways films get into trouble. Ridley is careful to have the writer around to contribute, though he probably needs one less than anybody."

Although he had access to the set, he stayed away "out of a kind of stunned superstition" during the actual shooting until they were in Seville. At that point he went down to the the Alcazar and watched Jeremy Irons and Brendan Gleeson do the scene in Tiberias' chambers that he describes in Chapter 1. That was when the realization hit of how far his own journey with *Kingdom of Heaven* had taken him.

Spells of hanging around were broken by spates of feverish action. "When we were shooting at Palacio del Portacarrero, an old Moorish fortress in Palma del Rio, I'd basically sit drinking coffee and working on the siege sequence, watching people drag camels past the windows of my trailer. But there was a fantastic moment when someone ran in and said, 'We need a scene to justify Balian's costume change.' So I wrote a scene in five minutes–the scene in which Godfrey, being carried in a litter, says, 'I don't want him fed in the kitchens.' I thought it was a terrific scene, sent it off–and heard nothing. I sat around wondering if Ridley liked it, then finally went down to the set. As he was coming out through some archway, I said, 'Did you like it, was it all right?' and he said, 'Already shot it, mate.'

"Of course, you can also fail. In Essaouira [a seaside location in Morocco] I ran down to redo the dialog between Guy and Balian but came up with nothing better. Then everyone realized that the existing bit was okay with a slight modification or omission."

Monahan recalls an evening when he returned to his trailer to find an unshaven fellow sitting on the step. He thought at first it was one of the Spanish workers, but in fact it was Orlando Bloom, "with a bit of paper and some questions about dialog. So we went through his notes and talked about the whole film." Occasionally Monahan was asked to help interpret the story for an actor, but Scott usually handled this, to keep signals clear.

Above: Scott and camera. Right: Balian and the Hospitaler.

"Everyone understood their parts and loved them, for which I was grateful," says the writer. "I became great friends with many of the actors in Spain and in the desert. It's really something, your first time out, to have David Thewlis and Jeremy Irons and Liam Neeson tell you that you've written a good script."

Monahan learned everything he could from everyone he met. Of the actor who plays Saladin, he says, "Ghassan Massoud is a brilliant man who did a fantastic Saladin, and he pleased me very much by saying that he thought the script would begin a new kind of dialog between Arabs and the West."

The Soul of a Knight

If Bill Monahan's experience on *Kingdom of Heaven* sounds like the fulfillment of an aspiring screenwriter's dream, he would agree. "I was given by Ridley, and seized with both hands, a chance to do a historical drama on the highest possible level—which Ridley then protected against all the pressures that can be brought to bear on a script or a writer in this business. Being able to write a film of this magnitude while operating full-bore as a literary artist—which I was generally allowed to do—while adjusting myself to the exigencies of film at this level, was an extraordinary opportunity. I attacked ambitiously and wrote about themes highly personal to me. Ridley was a lion in defense of the picture and of me, the best imaginable employer and counselor."

The film's essential theme could hardly have been more personal to Monahan, as it came from something his dying father said to him, quoting Mark's Gospel: "What does it profit a man to gain the whole world and lose his immortal soul?" The son realized that his father had thought about that question his entire life, and had always lived by the idea of doing the right thing. "I made that the 'soul' of Balian's knighthood," he says.

"The film proposes that it's better to live together than to be at war. That reason is better than fanaticism. That kindness is better than hate. That it's better to discard the world—money, position, power, whatever your times are telling you to do—than to endanger your integrity. If that gets across, then I did my job."

Casting the Kingdom

In gathering the players who would enact Ridley Scott's Crusades epic, both freedom and constraints were factors. The casting team was free to seek their featured actors from among the world's best, wherever they were to be found. Rather than star power, the film would be carried by its director's vision, its awe-some scope, its strong story, and performances shaped to that story's needs.

But there were real constraints too: first among them being a loudly ticking clock. Scott had committed to begin filming in January 2004 but could not turn his attention to casting until other key production decisions were made. By then it was early autumn. Budget constraints limited Scott to using just a handful of SAG actors. Still other factors were self-imposed: Scott was determined to focus on actors who would be most effective and believable in portraying medieval Europeans. Most challenging of all, he wanted all the Muslim characters in speaking roles to be played by Muslim actors, preferably by actors from the Middle East.

Two casting directors were hired: Debra Zane in Los Angeles and Jina Jay in London. Zane sourced prospects for all the key characters, though her main focus was identifying candidates who could play Balian. This pivotal choice would influence much of the other casting. "We started work in July and saw a lot of people," recalls Zane. "I was

delighted to get things started with Ridley—it had been a joy to work with him on *Matchstick Men*. But when we realized the shoot would be entirely overseas, it made sense to shift the main casting effort to Europe."

To Jay fell most of the work of casting European and Arab actors. It turned out to be the assignment of a lifetime, even for a professional who had cut her teeth in the business working with directors such as John Boorman and Mike Figgis.

"This was my first movie with Ridley," she notes. "*Alien* was one of three movies that made a deep impression on me as a teenager. So to work with him closely so many years later was a great thrill. Ridley was an amazing collaborator, very generous with me and with his time. I loved the script, and for me—I'm half Sri Lankan—it was an extraordinary opportunity to cast so many multi-ethnic and nonwhite roles."

Not that her work was easy. Shortly after she came on in October, Scott returned to London for an intensive casting period. "One really did sit and debate actor after actor, and what they could bring to roles. It wasn't an easy screenplay to cast," Jay notes, "because it's so layered with relationships. Whether the roles were small or large, even day players, everyone was significant. The connections amongst the characters were very complex."

By the time Scott and Jay began work in London, Orlando Bloom had been cast as Balian after an intensive search process. Debbie Zane showed Scott tape after tape of candidates, recalls producer Lisa Ellzey, but he struggled over who could most convincingly portray the character's journey from a naïve young artisan to the heroic defender of Jerusalem. Bloom's largest roles to date, in *Lord of the Rings, Pirates of the Caribbean*, and *Troy*, hadn't demanded the kind of multilayered performance he would be called on to deliver here. Bloom's journey growing into the role is described later; suffice it to say that his preparation and performance put all doubts to rest.

Casting at the Edge

None of the other principals could be cast until the Balian question was resolved, so Jay and her colleagues still faced a huge task: finding the ideal actors for complex roles, for a shoot due to begin in less than three months. Working for them were the "Ridley factor"—performers would go to great lengths to work with him—and a script that attracted all the actors who read it, even if some were attracted to parts other than those they were offered.

"Every actor we approached wanted to be in this picture," says Jay, "but some were only available for very limited period or at certain times, which made it all a great puzzle to put together." Scott's experienced and persistent producers, Terry Needham and Ellzey, had to precisely calibrate a character's time in front of the cameras and juggle schedules creatively to make the pieces fit. "Rather than lose an actor we wanted, they would do anything to make it work," says Jay. In this way, extremely busy actors such as Liam Neeson and Jeremy Irons could be accommodated in the shooting schedule.

The studio gave Scott plenty of leeway here, as elsewhere. Notes Jay, "So often with films on such a big scale, no one will entertain risks in relation to the schedule: unless actors are completely available and sensible picture deals can be done, forget it. But we were able to work much closer to the edge."

One of Jay's first moves was to consult with casting directors from France and Egypt, knowing she had to spread her net wide to pull in many prospects quickly, "especially on the non-English side." The Crusaders, of course, hailed from every part of Europe, and Scott wanted to represent a variety of types and accents in casting them. Among the European actors are Ulrich Thomsen (Templar Master), Nikolaj Coster-Waldau (Godfrey's nephew), Jouko Ahola (Odo), and Velibor Topic (Almaric). "I had done some casting from Europe before, and we ended up using a lot of theater actors, especially from Paris—I like casting from the theater and it worked for the script."

Sibylla, princess of Jerusalem and descendant of Frankish aristocracy, is fittingly played by a young French actress, Eva Green. Jay had heard about Green's debut in Bernardo Bertolucci's *The Dreamers*. "Though it wasn't yet released, the English agent who looked after Eva got me into a screening. Based on that, I brought her to London for a test, and Ridley met her." Again, because the

RIGHT: Ridley Scott and Jeremy Irons on the set in Morocco.

role was so crucial, the choice was much debated, but Jay stood firm in her commitment to the French newcomer and "eventually it was Eva."

It was in sourcing Arab actors that Jay's associates proved most helpful. "We did quickly find wonderful Arab actors in France, Germany, Belgium, all over Europe—but we needed to go further. We wanted the best actors in the world for these parts, especially Saladin, so we had to go directly to the Arab world."

The Mullah who is Saladin's chief advisor, for example, is played by Egyptian actor Khaled Nabwey, a major star in his homeland—"the Tom Cruise of Egypt," as Lisa Ellzey puts it. He accepted the relativelly small role in *Kingdom* for the sake of working with Ridley Scott. Nasser Memarzia, who plays a Muslim grandee, is another story: the Iranian-born actor and writer lives in England; has worked in stage, film, and TV; and teaches performing arts at Oxford and Cherwell College.

Fluency in English was a must, notes Jay. "Some of the most talented actors we saw don't speak English, so we couldn't touch them. Some whom we did use were coached—not because they didn't understand English perfectly, just to lighten or soften the accent to make sure they could be understood. Ridley's not interested in dubbing his actors."

The single greatest challenge was finding the right actor for Saladin, and it came down to the wire. Jay met with Egyptian casting director Nashwa Al-Ruwaini, who held casting sessions in Cairo, Damascus, Beirut, and Morocco, and sent Jay a large selection of videotapes of subtitled films. "I sat for hours and watched them without understanding a word, but the power and spirit of certain actors caught my attention." She made descriptive notes through which Al-Ruwaini identified the actors and then arranged for them to be taped. Among those tapes sent to Jay was one of Ghassan Massoud, a star of the stage and film in his native Syria.

Just before the New Year, Massoud and two other actors were flown to Spain, where Scott was hours away from beginning his shoot. Says Jay, "It very quickly emerged that Ghassan would be our Saladin."

Jay compares the process of casting *Kingdom of Heaven* to "painting an amazing picture—adding layer after layer of color." She feels immensely proud of her involvement on this work of art. "The actors were passionate about the material, and about Ridley as the director; it all made sense to them. There was an enormous sharing of commitment that went both ways."

BALIAN
Orlando Bloom

In the vast sweep of the Crusades, Balian of Ibelin is a relatively minor figure: not one of the princes who led armies across the Mediterranean to rescue the Holy Land, nor one of the kings who ruled there for a time. He was a vassal of King Baldwin IV and of the earlier kings who held the throne of Jerusalem—in fact, several generations of men named Balian were masters of this Crusader domain, which lay due west of Jerusalem, near the coast.

Still, the Balian who caught the imaginations of Ridley Scott and Bill Monahan stands out in the chronicles of his day—not for any vivid account left of his character or person, but from what can be read into his actions. He is a knight of noble blood who fought bravely at the Battle of the Horns of Hattin and survived: he is valorous. He seeks Saladin's leave to return to Jerusalem to look after his wife—from which one could infer that he is a loving spouse, a keen judge of men (Saladin grants his petition), or perhaps both. On arriving there, he takes command of the city's defense—he is a natural leader who inspires loyalty—but he also conveys his regrets to Saladin for breaking his parole: a man of honor. He is practical when need calls: fortifying and provisioning the town against a siege, knighting common men and boys to swell the ranks of armed defenders. And he is quick-witted and resourceful: when it appears that Saladin must overwhelm the defenses and lay waste to Jerusalem, Balian stalemates him by threatening ruin to the city's holy places and its Muslim population.

From these essential ingredients of character, the filmmakers create a hero to suit their purposes. The film's Balian merges with the historical Balian after a long journey of discovery that begins in France. His coming of age proceeds through several stages: loss and despair at the deaths of his wife and child; hope for redemption through a pilgrimage to the Holy Land; and transformation—initiated when he is bequeathed the rights and responsibilities of knighthood. His conduct when he reaches Palestine—from running his estate to his

choices with Sibylla to his last stand on Jerusalem's walls—all spring from his slowly acquired sense of what a knight should be.

It's not stretching a point to say that Orlando Bloom went through a transformative journey of his own to portray Balian. His previous film roles showed him as a youth or an immortal warrior free of human passions. But in *Kingdom of Heaven*, he is the crux of the story's emotions, actions, and soul. For the film to work, audiences must believe in Balian and care about what he does.

Bloom first met Ridley Scott when he took a small part in *Black Hawk Down* (2002), as a soldier who falls from the helicopter and thus sets off the doomed rescue attempt. Scott saw promise in him then, but he had a lot of growing up to do to fulfill the director's vision of Balian.

Bloom's preparation required a great deal of physical training, beginning with adding weight and muscle to his slight frame. A good rider since childhood, he was well equipped for the horseback work in *Kingdom*, but he had to hone his swordplay and learn blacksmithing skills. Vocal training was also part of the package: Scott wanted him to use a deeper, more mature voice for Balian. "Ridley turned Orlando into a leading man with his work for this film," says Lisa Ellzey. "Orlando should be proud of both the hard work and the results."

Scott, who became something of a father figure to Bloom in the course of the production, had faith his lead actor could pull it off. "We needed a hero—someone who could fit into the shoes and spurs of the character we had written," he says. "And Orlando certainly fulfills that. He has an honesty and integrity that are really built in, and which come through in his performance."

Bloom is the first to acknowledge his good fortune in winning this role at this point in his career. "It's an incredible arc for a character: starting out as a sort of reluctant hero and eventually becoming defender of Jerusalem. Having the opportunity to do my first leading role with Ridley Scott and to be a part of all this... it's something I'm still pinching myself about, really."

SIBYLLA
Eva Green

Sibylla, princess of Jerusalem, is an ambiguous figure in history. Although she apparently was devoted to her younger brother, King Baldwin IV, she acted against his wishes and gave her love foolishly. In taking a second husband after the death of her son's father, she chose not one of the strong, responsible lords proposed by Baldwin, but the vain, ambitious, and incompetent Guy de Lusignan. Her young son became Baldwin V after the king's death, but the boy himself soon died. Sibylla was crowned queen but, still blindly attached to Guy, passed the crown to him, with disastrous consequences for the kingdom.

As redrawn for the screenplay, Sibylla is differently made: just as passionate but more clear-sighted. Here, Guy is her first husband, chosen by her family when she was fifteen, and she has come to detest him. Balian's forthright charm and quiet strength win her heart, though she hides her feelings out of political caution. As the story darkens, her actions express her strong sense of duty, fierce family loyalty, and love for her homeland.

Sibylla, when Balian meets her, is a splendid, imperious creature, the kind of wild child one might expect in a European princess raised on a desert frontier—happiest with her horses and dogs but elegantly civilized when she chooses. Eva Green's portrayal fully captures this quality, feels Jina Jay. "She really is a kind of creature, with a powerful soul—not quite a dark soul, but there's something almost preternatural about her. She operates on a very instinctual level."

Convincing everyone that Green was the right choice took a while, however. Her only other major film role had been her remarkable debut in Bertolucci's *The Dreamers* (2003), though she had considerable theater experience in France, as well as training at London's Webber Douglas acting school (accounting in part for her excellent English). The Paris native has movie genes as well; her mother is the actress Marlène Joubert.

Says Jay, "It didn't feel like a gamble at all, because I knew she was right. Ridley and I fought very hard for her. But it's a big picture and a lot was riding on her, for an actress with not very much experience. It's tough walking onto a set like that, where there are no other significant female roles—so she is carrying a great deal. And she carries it off beautifully."

GODFREY OF IBELIN
Liam Neeson

Unlike most of the principals, Godfrey has no specific counterpart in history. The film's Godfrey of Ibelin gives us the picture of a Crusader knight who is typical in some ways: the younger son of a provincial Frankish lord, he saw the Holy Land as an opportunity—and so it proved, as he became a baron and landholder there. As we meet him, he has returned home (as some Crusaders did from time to time) to check up on his family's fortunes and probably to recruit men to his service.

Godfrey has a more unusual mission, however. Although not a conventionally pious man, Godfrey tries to keep faith with the knight's code of right action. So for reasons buried deep in his past, he seeks out the young blacksmith of his feudal village. In a complex scene set in Balian's forge, he offers Balian the opportunity to journey back to the East with him, and employment on his estate in Ibelin. Thus the film's primary action is set in motion, and during that journey Godfrey comes to recognize Balian as a man worthy of his title and trust.

Godfrey is among the most loyal vassals of King Baldwin, who badly needs such able defenders. A man of the world, he has no use for religious intolerance, and though adept at war shares Baldwin's vision of peace. These facts will seal Balian's own destiny in the Kingdom of Jerusalem, because Godfrey on the journey knights Balian, making him swear to serve the king and fight for the peace.

Since his Oscar-nominated performance in *Schindler's List* (1993), Irish-born star Liam Neeson is more often seen in leading roles (the latest being Bill Condon's *Kinsey*), but the chance to work with Ridley Scott on a film story of depth and substance gave him incentive enough to come on board. He recognized that Godfrey was a crucial role because he must establish a relationship with Balian

quickly and believably—and because of what he stands for as a true knight.

"The challenge," as Neeson describes it, "was to portray a man who earned his living from fighting and all that encompasses, and yet to have a sensitivity to the idea that Christian and Muslim have to live together. Godfrey has come to this realization only after many years of senseless killing. And then he must somehow get through to Balian, whom he's just met—convince him to come out to Jerusalem, and that there is a way forward for all of us.

"That's pretty weighty stuff, but it was made easier by Ridley. This whole complex story just seemed to move like a well-oiled machine from day one, because of him."

While earlier period roles such as *Rob Roy* had given him experience in riding and swordfighting, Neeson appreciated the brush-up training he received for this job, and discovered that performing in suits of armor was a major new test. Yet his most important preparation was for the more intimate acting, he says. "We started off very simply with the scenes between Orlando and myself, just reading and getting a feel for the words."

Neeson enjoyed the balance in *Kingdom* between rousing entertainment and serious purpose. "There's a lot of action in true Ridley Scott style; he doesn't skimp on the horses and the manpower and the swords being wielded. So it's very exciting. But it's also rooted in a reality that was very complex and that did change the world. We're still feeling the effects of the Crusades to this day, with great mutual mistrust and confusion and ignorance between Muslim and Christian. I think this film goes some way towards explaining that confusion and showing where these wars came from."

TIBERIAS
Jeremy Irons

The knight and lord known as Tiberias in the script is King Baldwin's most faithful lieutenant, a perceptive and skillful diplomat who shares the king's goal of maintaining peace with Saladin and works with all his might toward that goal. This character hews closely to his historical model, whose name was actually Raymond of Tripoli. It was clear, though, that this name was too easily confused with Reynald, another knight—and furthermore, "Tripoli" was associated with a different Scott-Monahan project. So the character played by Jeremy Irons was called Tiberias, actually the name of Raymond's stronghold and estate, which figures importantly in the downfall of Jerusalem.

Tiberias is mine and the Lady of Tiberias is my wife, and our children are in the castle together with all our possessions, and if it falls, no one will lose as much as I. I know that if the Saracens... take my wife and my children and my possessions, I can ransom them back again. If they attack my city, I shall in time make it strong again. And to me there is more advantage that Tiberias be taken... than that this entire land should be lost to us. For I know that if you go to the help of Tiberias, you will all be taken or killed, you and all your army.

—RAYMOND OF TRIPOLI, ARGUING TO KING GUY AND THE BARONS WHY THEY SHOULD NOT MARCH OUT TO RESCUE HIS OWN CASTLE. THEY FAILED TO HEED HIS ADVICE AND WERE DESTROYED AT HATTIN.

While Baldwin IV was still a boy king, Raymond of Tripoli served as his guardian. One historian describes him as "an impressive character, hard, reserved, efficient, and capable of prompt action. ... In the feverish court of the leper king, which was full of intrigues, [his] gift of equanimity was especially valuable." He served the king well, yet helped sow the seeds of the kingdom's destruction by fatally alienating a powerful Templar knight.

When Baldwin knew he was dying, he appointed Raymond as regent, this time for his young nephew. This temporarily staved off Guy de Lusignan's grab for the throne, but only until the young king died. Even then some of the barons contested Guy (and Sibylla's) claim, preferring the capable Raymond as their leader against a resur-

gent Saladin. But Guy had the Templars and the Patriarch of Jerusalem in his camp, and prevailed.

The screenplay's portrait of Tiberias is remarkably faithful to Raymond's history. In scene after scene, he parries the moves of the bloodthirsty Reynald and the ambitious Guy; at the end, when all is lost, he retreats to the island of Cyprus—as did the real Raymond.

Clearly the part called for an actor of great presence and subtlety, and the filmmakers were thrilled to secure their unquestioned first choice. Limited to a brief few weeks on the set, Irons had to set down his scenes quickly and efficiently. His no-nonsense work ethic won admiration from all the other cast and crew, as did his willingness to modulate his own powerful acting style as needed to balance his scenes with the younger leads.

SALADIN
Ghassan Massoud

A prime motive for dramatizing this particular period of the Crusades was the chance to feature the great sultan and general Saladin. A preeminent hero of Islam and mostly admired by Western historians as well, he is a more complex figure than any film portrait can fully capture. But for Scott it was an irresistible invitation.

"A lot has been made of the film's presenting Saladin in a positive light," notes Scott. "But it isn't hard to do. He's regarded as probably the next greatest Muslim after Mohammed—a great strategist, leader, warrior, politician, and intellect. So it was easy to start thinking of him in heroic terms." Scott can't predict if the film's portrait of Saladin will promote understanding of the Muslim view-

point on the Crusades; he does hope it conveys some of the man's stature and charisma.

How well it does that hangs on the performance, of course. Ghassan Massoud is among the most respected stage and film actors in his native Syria and throughout the Arab world. He has a strong background in Islamic history and has worked on many historical drama series. Physically he bears a close resemblance to descriptions handed down of Saladin.

Massoud is well aware of the privilege of portraying his culture's legendary hero. "It is a very, very special experience for me, as it would be for any actor from our country. Saladin is a very rich memory for the Islamic and for the whole Arab world. First of all, he is a statesman. Second, he is a man of war, the winner in many battles. But at the same time he made dialogue with the enemy. It's an important point for leaders today.

"Because he is from my culture, I can understand him. I can imagine how this man thinks about himself, about statesmanship, about war, about making dialogue, about love and women. So it's not a strange character for me."

Like any good actor Massoud also welcomed the chance to work with Scott. "In the East we know Ridley Scott well from his films. We know that he is a very special director, and we respect him–how he thinks about this film and about how to build the characters."

Most of all he is eager to make audiences better acquainted with Saladin, to show him as a complete character rather than just an icon. "Who is this man, really? We know that he is a good leader; he is charismatic. He knows how to make policy. If we can show all these parts of him, I think we can make a good impact with audiences in West and East."

Saladin Behind the Mask

If Scott faces criticism from Western critics for the film's harsh view of some Christian Crusaders, some Arabs fear it may perpetuate negative stereotyping of the Islamic world. Ghassan Massoud is in effect the film's point man within his own culture, and well before *Kingdom*'s release had fielded several interviews. His comments below are taken from a conversation with the *Syria Times*.

"As soon as I got a call to meet the director, I had concerns about any negativity towards Arabs and Muslims in the film, because I can't participate in something like that.

"I have read many books and references about Saladin, but I think that we usually deal with a historical figure as a mask. In Arab drama we tend to paint a historical figure that does no wrong. In reading the film's script, I kept in mind that we can't provide the audience with a sterile historical character.

"My opinion is that behind the mask we love and respect there's a lot to be known. Saladin's charisma and how he appears before his soldiers and people is the mask, but what would we see if we follow him to his tent and find him all by himself?

"I found that the character has a high degree of balance in the story, and a great deal of respect from the screenwriter and the director. I am not exaggerating when I say that my thoughts and the director's thoughts about Saladin were nearly identical. Ridley Scott proved that he respects Saladin and strongly admires the chivalry and nobility of the man."

THE HOSPITALER
David Thewlis

The character played by English actor David Thewlis is known only as the Hospitaler. The name derives from one of the most important "military orders" to arise out of the Crusades: ordained clerics who were also fighting knights and who had much to do with running the Kingdom of Jerusalem.

The name, as Ridley Scott points out, "comes from hospital and hospitality. As played by David Thewlis, this character is an impressive figure: a samaritan, a doctor, a warrior, and a priest, which makes him formidable. He speaks with the voice of reason and right behavior, saying to Balian, 'It's all right if you don't hear the voice of God; you can still be a good man.'"

The Hospitaler has no direct historical model; he was really created, as writer Monahan notes, to show the Christian tradition in its best light, in contrast to some other Crusaders. He serves as Godfrey of Ibelin's personal confessor and spiritual mentor. Later, the Hospitaler becomes Balian's counselor and friend.

David Thewlis is probably best known to American audiences for his role as Professor Remus Lupin in the third installment of the Harry Potter series. But the versatile actor has delivered memorable performances in many films, including those of Mike Leigh. Thewlis has also directed (winning a BAFTA nomination for his first short film) and pursues music and writing fiction and poetry.

GUY DE LUSIGNAN
Marton Csokas

One of a pair of authentic villains in *Kingdom of Heaven* is Guy de Lusignan, whose character closely parallels the historical Guy: a French aristocrat who marries King Baldwin's sister Sibylla, eventually becomes king himself, and promptly loses Jerusalem after the great defeat at Hattin.

Historians see Guy chiefly as a lady's man and flatterer, easily led by stronger personalities such as Reynald of Chatillon and the hawkish Templars. But the film emphasizes his calculated striving for power, especially his extreme antipathy to Balian—whom he recognizes as competition for Sibylla's affection as well as for the loyalty of lords and subjects. In having Sibylla reject Guy as a husband, the script makes him all the more interesting and arouses our sympathy. But his pride is stronger

When Guy heard that he had been disinherited [by his wife's son], he wreaked his vengeance not on the dying king but on some harmless Arab shepherds who, under the king's protection, pastured their flocks outside the castle of Daron. He captured the shepherds, seized the flocks and drove them all to Ascalon. It was his way of telling the king, "You cannot protect anyone."

— Robert Payne, *The Dream and the Tomb*

than his love for her: when he sees his path to power, he tries to blackmail her.

Marton Csokas (pronounced Cho-karsh) may be the most culturally blended actor in this international cast: his father is Hungarian and his mother from New Zealand, where he grew up and embarked on a stage career. He won his spurs as an action hero during several seasons of playing Borias in *Xena: Warrior Princess.* A gifted actor on the verge of becoming a leading man, Csokas gives a full-blooded, nuanced portrayal of Guy that will make audiences sit up and take notice.

REYNALD OF CHATILLON
Brendan Gleeson

Reynald is the second of the film's well-rounded villains: a powerful, headstrong lord who is dedicated to Christian domination of the Holy Land and to improving his own fortunes, in about equal parts. Although at one time he served as regent for the disabled Baldwin IV, he defied the king's truce with Saladin and so helped bring down the kingdom. His unceasing provocation of Muslims—especially raiding their caravans—was largely responsible for Saladin's invasion. Reynald even cherished ambitions to march into Arabia and sack Mecca itself.

Reynald's extremism might be traced partly to the vulnerable position of his domains on the far eastern frontiers of the kingdom: his castle at Kerak was threatened several times by Saladin's forces, as depicted in one episode of the film. But temperamentally he was certainly a man inclined to warring. In the screenplay, when Guy says to him: "Give me a war, Reynald," the latter replies simply, "That is what I do."

Dublin-born Brendan Gleeson is yet another in *Kingdom*'s distinguished roster of veterans, an actor of great force and range. He gained wide attention in Mel Gibson's *Braveheart* and has since taken many period roles—recently as King Menelaus in *Troy*.

IMAD
Alexander Siddig

Another character invented for the story's purposes is the young Muslim knight Imad, Saladin's confidant and commander of his cavalry. He serves as a kind of Arab counterpart to Balian: similar in age, intelligent, honorable, and humane. He is the first person Balian encounters after the shipwreck that lands him on the shore of Palestine, and Imad escorts the Frenchman into Jerusalem. Although he hides his true identity from Balian then, it's revealed when they meet later in the story.

While Imad is fictional, his name (and to some extent his character) is an homage to the eloquent Muslim chronicler Imad ad-Din, who accompanied Saladin on his expeditions and reported on the Battle of Hattin. In the screenplay Imad is described as "scholarly" in appearance, and we might imagine that he will one day set down his own history of Saladin's campaigns.

Alexander Siddig, one of the Muslim actors cast by Scott in featured roles, was born in the Sudan (as Siddig El Fadil) but has spent most of his life in England. His first film role led to his being cast as

Dr. Julian Bashir in the TV series *Star Trek: Deep Space Nine*, in which he appeared for several seasons, becoming a favorite among "Trekkies."

PATRIARCH OF JERUSALEM
Jon Finch

The face of religion at its most politicized and hypocritical is represented in *Kingdom of Heaven* by the Patriarch of Jerusalem—the kingdom's chief prelate, whose historical name was Heraclius.

As described by historian Robert Payne, "He had reached his high position by intrigue; he was barely literate but wielded enormous powers. He was especially close to Guy de Lusignan, Reynald of Chatillon, and the members of the young, new nobility." Heraclius was part of Guy's faction and supported him in his claim to the throne on the death of Sibylla's son.

Left in charge of Jerusalem when Guy and his knights marched out to their doom at Hattin, he was "distrusted by its inhabitants, and detested by the clergy and the captains of the garrisons," who were thus more than ready to give their allegiance to Balian of Ibelin when he returned to lead the defense. When the city fell, the Patriarch paid the ten pieces of gold that Saladin demanded of every man as a freedom price, and then absconded with much of the city's treasure: gold plate from the churches, even from the Church of the Holy Sepulchre. When Saladin, a pious man, was told of this he refused to intervene and forbade anyone from harming Heraclius.

The filmmakers show no such mercy in their portrait of the Patriarch. Given a choice, he always does what is most expedient and likely to ensure his own survival. In one of his several confrontations with Balian during the siege of Jerusalem, he suggests that they both flee the city, leaving its people to their fate. In another scene he tries to stop Balian from burning the bodies of those killed, claiming it will damn their souls. To which Balian replies, "God will understand, my lord Heraclius. And if he doesn't understand, then he isn't God and we needn't worry about him." Balian's final ironic comment to the Patriarch is, "You have taught me a great deal about religion."

The veteran English character actor Jon Finch, best known in title role of Roman Polanski's *The Tragedy of Macbeth* (1971), plays the Patriarch.

Part 2

Swords and Stones

How *Kingdom of Heaven* Was Made

Producing the Impossible

Ridley Scott set himself a large task with *Kingdom of Heaven*. He had committed to beginning principal photography in January 2004, just five months after the deal was made–and to deliver the movie just over a year later.

There were good reasons for the hard target to begin shooting. Scott knew that November would be a difficult time to be on location in Morocco, because of Muslim workers observing the Ramadan festival. He needed to catch the winter snow at his main Spanish location. And he didn't dare begin later than January, because by June, shooting under the blistering Saharan sun becomes unbearable–especially for men in armor and their horses. They had to wrap by then.

Five months to ready a big period production for shooting sounds absurd, with all the research and sourcing of locations, crew, sets, and costumes. But Scott had worlds of experience in such undertakings. His background in commercials, with their four-week cycle from start to finish, schooled him to believe that anything is doable on a tight schedule. By his own admission, he likes to work fast. And he had a few magic arrows in his quiver.

For one thing he had recently been through the process of identifying locations, crew, and other resources for the *Tripoli* production, which then had to be sidelined. *Kingdom*, he realized, could make good use of infrastructure that had already been set up for the other film, and some of the same locations in Morocco.

But more than anything, Scott's confidence rested in the seasoned and dedicated people who stood ready to respond when he picked up the phone. From his energetic producers to the creative heads who worked on many of his previous films (production designer Arthur Max, cinematographer John Mathieson, film editor Dody Dorn, costume designer Janty Yates), these professionals possessed the talents, connections, and steel nerves it would take to get *Kingdom of Heaven* ready for the cameras.

"You need a few key people you're in synch with," Scott confirms. "You're always taking on new units, up to 450 people–so I go with certain personnel, the guys I call to say, 'Okay, I'm thinking about this'–and they spring into action. There's an automatic ethic of research. Everyone leaps in and is very well prepared."

Most closely involved in getting (and keeping) the production up and running were executive producers Lisa Ellzey, Branko Lustig, and Terry Needham. Ellzey, as president of Scott Free, held the fort in the company's Los Angeles office, tracking ongoing script work and scheduling issues, liaising with the studio, and continuing to develop and produce other projects for the company. She visited the Morocco locations for meetings and to help document the unfolding production.

"Communication was key because there were so many people in so many countries," she says. "Eventually we would have production offices in London, L.A., Spain, and Morocco, as well as art departments in Rome and Madrid. Roman Polanski once said that you can make a movie without film but not without a telephone. Today I'd add the same thing about email and faxes."

Branko Lustig oversaw the film's finances and budgeting, acted as liaison with officials in every country where they would shoot film or do business, and was most responsible for coordinating the constant flow of materials and equipment. If the film needed 400 camels, a dozen heavy trucks, or a new road into a location, he could make it happen somehow. The Croatian-born Lustig began his film career in Europe, where he worked on the mega-miniseries *The Winds of War* and *War and Remembrance* for television. He helped Steven Spielberg produce *Schindler's List* in 1993, and it was Spielberg who recommended him to Scott when the latter was seeking help with his multi-location work on *Gladiator*. Since then he has been Scott's executive producer on *Hannibal, Black Hawk Down,* and now *Kingdom*.

Both *Kingdom of Heaven* and *Gladiator* used locations in Europe and Morocco to tell stories of grand sweep. But as Arthur Max points

ABOVE: Executive producer Lisa Ellzey and props. RIGHT: Executive producer Branko Lustig. PRECEDING PAGES: The coronation scene was filmed in the Cathedral of Avila, in Spain.

You need a few key people you're in synch with. There's an automatic ethic of research. Everyone leaps in and is very well prepared.

—Ridley Scott

out, *Kingdom* was an even bigger challenge to design and mount. The Jerusalem set alone may be the largest free-standing set ever constructed for a modern movie (at least since *Ben-Hur*, he believes). And in this film, notes Max, "we're depicting a greater cross section of society. In fact, it's two whole societies: the Christian and Islamic, with their very different aesthetics and belief systems."

According to Lustig, the challenges of making *Kingdom* were "mostly behind the camera, what the audience doesn't see. Getting the sets made on time. And bringing hundreds of people to Morocco and servicing them all." He credits the experience of the crew, from the top down, for being able to prepare so quickly. "We called our crew from *Gladiator*, from *Black Hawk Down*, and people we had almost contracted with for *Tripoli*. And we just made it."

Lustig reels off an impressive array of production statistics. "We used about 25,000 to 30,000 extras, at all the locations. In Morocco we also had about 8,500 horse riders acting as cavalry for both sides. And a few hundred camel riders as well." He tips his ever-present hat to extras casting coordinator Billy Dowd, who hires the live bodies for the crowd scenes as well as bit parts and doubles. To match the film's multiethnic range, Dowd had to find Arabic-looking people in Spanish locations that subbed for the Holy Land, and European-looking faces in Morocco to play the westerners.

As for crew, they came from all around the world; the international crew brought to Morocco numbered 436. "We are also employing 443 Moroccans: that was the quota set by the government," says Lustig.

Morocco's government cooperated fully with the production, starting with King Mohammed VI, who read the script, approved financial arrangements, and gave the producers unprecedented access to resources. Most valuable was assistance from Morocco's army, which has many skilled cavalry officers. "They are very disciplined, and many bring their own horses," says Lustig. "And they already had some training for film work on *Alexander*. So they know how to take direction."

Sharing responsibility with Lustig for getting all the pieces in place is Terry Needham, whose work started with the crucial "crewing up": assembling its technical crew. One of Scott's oldest friends

Giraffe
FILMAIR

الله
الله
الله
Giraffe

and associates, Needham was first assistant director on nearly all Scott's films from *1492* to *Black Hawk Down*, as well as having associate producer credit on most. Before he became linked to Scott, he had been Stanley Kubrick's first A.D. on *Full Metal Jacket* and second A.D. on *The Shining*.

Needham has encyclopedic recall of every crew member he has ever worked with, and their loyalty to him and to Scott is intense. Among his key lieutenants was Adam Somner, another longtime Scott associate who had been second A.D. on *Gladiator* (and other major films), and made the jump to first A.D. on *Kingdom*, with Needham moving to executive producer. (Somner's more recent A.D. credits include *Seabiscuit* and Spielberg's 2005 remake of *War of the Worlds*.)

Once most crew assignments are filled, Needham moves into the role of scheduling master. The intricate plotting out of what happens

By the Numbers

Feet of film shot	1.2 million
Plaster "stonework" cast for walls of Jerusalem set, in tons	6,000
Individual molds cast from old found stonework	300
Extent of Jerusalem set walls, in square meters	28,000
People working on set construction in two countries	500
Different flag designs created	650
Budget for flags, in dollars	3,000
Shields made	3,000
Pieces of medieval horse tack made	1,250
Medieval forges built	12
12th-century bathtubs made	6
Fifty-foot siege towers built	3
Weight of each tower, in tons	25
Gas pipe laid around Jerusalem set for fire effects, in kilometers	1
Propane used for fire effects, in liters	120,000
Arrows made	20,000
Costumes created for extras	14,000

when involves him deeply in casting issues; planning for set construction, effects work, and other creative components; as well as the day-to-day conduct of the shoot. He's the person most responsible for planning the scope of each day's work as detailed on the call sheet.

"Scheduling for a production like this is really an art form, and Terry's brilliant at it," says Ellzey. "It requires knowing the director and exactly what he's capable of, how far to push a crew, which actors are available exactly when. He's aware of everything that's going on on the set at any given time."

Even before shooting begins, Scott, Needham, and colleagues engage in a kind of "pre-direction" process for key scenes, such as the siege of Jerusalem. In one or more meetings, they plan out all the logistics of filming. Needham makes sure that all key personnel for that scene are present–including Adam Somner and any department heads involved: perhaps Simon Atherton, the armorer; chief horse master Steve Dent; or practical and visual effects staff. Working with Scott's storyboards (which may have been drawn just prior), they lay out exactly how things will unfold: how many of these riders, how are they equipped, how high must the flames be? And of course the deployment of cameras, lighting, and sound equipment.

Throughout the shoot, as story changes occurred or conditions on the set demanded, new storyboards would emerge and ad hoc meetings would be held to bring everyone up to speed. Arthur Max notes that Ridley's ideas about how to shoot something often will coalesce only after he sees how a set actually takes shape.

Needham tends to brush off the idea that there's anything remarkable in what he does. To him the real story behind making *Kingdom of Heaven* lies in its startling conjuction of storyline, place, and timing. "Here we were, a production from two countries currently making war in a Moslem nation," (referring to the U.S. and Great Britain in Iraq), "shooting a story about holy wars in a devoutly Moslem country, Morocco."

That these factors seem to have generated almost no friction during the filmmaking is remarkable. The filmmakers were aware they were on sensitive ground, and took steps to ease possible concerns

PRECEDING PAGES: The crew films a dolly shot of Saracen cavalry charging at Kerak. ABOVE: Executive producer Terry Needham.

about the project in Morocco—starting with involving the king, whose acceptance carried considerable weight.

For a time, though, they did have a Plan B. "As producers we're responsible for the safety and well-being of our crew, and there were intense discussions about the political climate," says Needham. "We budgeted, scouted, and scheduled an alternative plan for Spain that involved more locations but less set-building, and pushed ahead on two fronts for a while—the Morocco set versus Jerusalem in Andalucia. But Branko got very positive signals from the Moroccan government, so finally we went ahead there."

For the many Muslims employed on the crew, the production made arrangements to accommodate dietary restrictions and prayer schedules. Ellzey remembers, on a visit to the set, seeing a group of extras costumed as Saladin's soldiers walk far out into the desert one by one and drop to their knees, facing east, to pray at sunset. (Islamic law does allow working people to skip prescribed prayer times while they are actively engaged in work.)

Ultimately Moroccan officials and crew members were happy to be connected with the film. They appreciated its complimentary treatment of Saladin and the balanced story line in general. The fact that Saladin was played by an Arab actor they all knew of and admired went a long way toward reinforcing their good opinion of the production.

"Nothing is without risk, especially in an action movie," notes Needham, "but our job is to minimize it. In this case the risk was connected with a geopolitical situation. But thanks to good diplomacy, all went remarkably well in Morocco."

Visions of the Past

The films of Ridley Scott are defined by their visual power and richly imagined worlds, whether set in the future (*Alien, Blade Runner*) or the past. Trained at the Royal College of Art, his style later forged by the discipline of advertising, Scott has been called "the greatest visual stylist working today" by fellow director Alan Parker.

Not surprising, then, that the Crusades as a film subject knocked around in his mind for years. Like any English lad, he grew up on romantic images of that era: the pageantry of banners and tented pavilions and coats-of-arms; the spectacle of mounted knights in a charge; battlemented fortresses and soaring palace walls; and the great, clanking machinery of medieval warfare.

When he began research for the film, new dimensions opened everywhere he looked. Especially toward the East: Scott relished the prospect of exploring the aesthetics of Arab and Muslim civilization of the period. He discovered how the Crusaders adopted the ways of their conquered land and left their own mark on it—in fortified castles all along the frontiers of the Holy Land. This blending of cultures is seen above all in Jerusalem, and Jerusalem would be the visual heart of Scott's film.

RIGHT: **Pilgrims Going to Mecca,** ***by Léon-Auguste-Adolphe Belly, 1861.***

The Art of Research

Scott and production designer Arthur Max—his colleague on *Gladiator* and several other films—met in June 2003, sat down and talked through the story: what kinds of locations would be required, what the key sets would be. Then Max did what he always does: plunged into research, mostly in books and museums. Having worked with him for nearly 20 years, Max knew how to look through Scott's eyes. The director had always favored the Romantic painters of the mid-19th century—painters like Delacroix and Jean-Léon Gérôme—for their intensification of reality, visual exaggeration, and dramatic lighting.

His search for images of the Crusades soon led Max to the *Musée du Château* (a museum of French history) in Versailles, outside Paris. "In it is the Salle de Croisades—five large rooms of commissioned historical paintings of Crusaders," says Max. The Salle was created in 1839 when French interest in their medieval history was being rekindled. Both Max and costume designer Janty Yates referred to paintings and heraldic imagery from this source over and over.

A subset of Romantic painters known as the Orientalists also helped shape the look of the production. After Napoleon conquered Egypt at the dawn of the 19th century, westerners began to stream into the Arab world for the first time. Among them were many artists, who painted daily life and buildings, as well as historical subjects. Western artists were amazed by the color of light in the Middle East and North Africa. Orientalist painters whose work Max brought to Scott's attention included Léon Belly (see preceding page) and Eugène Fromentin, of France, and the German August Löffler, whose long-range view of Jerusalem under a stormy sky was a key image for the film.

Max and Scott also looked at the highly charged black-and-white etchings of Gustave Doré, the mid-19th century French book illustrator. Doré won fame for his illustrations of Dante's *Inferno, Don Quixote*, and the Bible. His two-volume *Illustrations of the Crusades* provided ideas "especially for lighting," says Scott.

"The basic model for architecture was a layering of styles from these European painters that would give us a romantic imagined Jerusalem," says Max. "We don't try to duplicate the historical places with total fidelity, though where possible the general layout and many details are based on research. But like those 18th- and 19th-century painters who take license, Ridley's design usually intensifies or 'densifies' what's there."

LEFT: Detail of Jerusalem, *by August Löffler, 1853. This was one of Scott's chief inspirations for depicting Jerusalem in the film. TOP RIGHT: Detail of an etching of Saladin by Gustave Doré, 1877. RIGHT: Illustration from the* Encyclopédie Médiévale.

Different kinds of art were used for different purposes. Certain paintings were used as "benchmarks" for planning visual effects, or to suggest lighting, shadows and color palettes. Set dressing and costuming also leaned heavily on such sources.

"It's all in service of one man's vision," observes Max. "For example, when we first talked about the set for Kerak (Reynald of Chatillon's castle), Ridley wanted a fortress on an imposing hilltop with great plain below, and huge imposing gates. In the real Kerak the gates were quite small, for practical reasons, but what we're doing is more like a theater set on film. The huge gates were meant to impress, to intimidate and evoke mood and emotion; the scene is more operatic than archeological."

Of course, Scott's visual memory is full of images from films that have made an impact on him. He has acknowledged the influence of Kurosawa and Bergman in forming his desire to show knighthood on film, and certain details have found their way into *Kingdom of Heaven*. "The model for Balian's forge was a little building in Bergman's *Virgin Spring,* I think," Scott recalls.

In the early stages of production design, Max and his art department assemble a large scrapboard of reference material: photographs of actual places, tearsheets from books of paintings or graphic art, and the director's sketches. This reference wall is constantly reshuffled and updated as Scott reviews and edits his ideas. When the production moved to Spain and then Morocco, the wall went along. It was all part of the ongoing visual dialogue the director and his staff engage in.

As they looked and talked and drew and looked some more, visual themes began to emerge. The film would begin in Europe with cool, wintry tones and explode into warmth, sunlight, and strong color when Balian reached the Near East. They would seek to mingle Western and Eastern architectural styles in the film's built environments, to reflect the experience of Europeans in the Holy Land.

What places could they find to serve as settings, with or without some structural "editing" by the production? What places would they need to create from scratch, or partially create and then enhance with film technology? Those were the next questions, which they had to leave their offices to answer.

On Location

The script gave Scott and his team their targets for location scouting. They needed to re-create a village attached to a lord's castle in medieval France, and certain places on the road to the Holy Land. Once the story moved to the Near East, action would occur on the coastline where Balian washes up after being shipwrecked, at his rural estate of Ibelin, at Reynald's imposing fortress of Kerak, and throughout old Jerusalem.

"We set off scouting in Spain and Morocco within days after Ridley first contacted me in June," recalls Arthur Max. "and were having meetings back in L.A. within a matter of weeks." There was very little time for scouting, so Max and executive producer Terry Needham split up in Spain, Max taking the northern region and Needham the south. Later in the summer they made a trip to Morocco, where they already had strong motivations for shooting.

Perhaps surprisingly, they scouted the Holy Land only in pictures, using books and other documentation of the period. "Jerusalem is a modern city now," Max observes. "There's too much visual clutter to get much useful information on camera. We also knew that the practical realities of shooting there would be beyond our reach."

As for other sites around the Near East, such as the fortress of Kerak, the filmmakers knew there was little to be gained by taking time to visit in person. "Many historic structures are in ruins or too fragile to have a film crew around," says Max. "It was better to re-create what we wanted based on our research into how they looked in medieval times, as well as buildings from that period in other places."

Location scouting photos of Fint Oasis (top) and Ait Ben Haddou (bottom), near Ouarzazate. TOP RIGHT: *Scouting photo of desert landscape near Fint.* BOTTOM RIGHT: *Moulay Beach, near Essaouira, where the shipwreck scene was filmed.*

Their journeys turned up a wide range of locations in Spain and Morocco that met the story's diverse requirements. In Spain, particularly, they discovered many places where European and Arab influences met and mingled, due to the long Moorish occupation of the peninsula.

To their great satisfaction, the filmmakers found one location in northeastern Spain that could do full service as Balian's village in France, including its feudal castle—Godfrey's ancestral home, now held by his brother. This was the Castle of Loarre in the foothills of the Pyrénées, about seven hours' drive north of Madrid. (The closest town was Huesca, about an hour away.) Dating from the late 11th and early 12th centuries, nearly contemporaneous with the film's story, Loarre offered wonderful exterior views of its well-preserved main keep and an interior hall that could serve as the lord's dining hall.

Outside at the foot of the castle a large field sloped away downhill, empty of all but a coffee stand for tourists. There they could build sets for the village, including Balian's forge, which could be effectively shot from the castle walls above. Those sets would go up during the autumn so that the film's wintry opener could be shot there in January.

Moving west- and southward through Spain, the ancient cities of Segovia and Avila offered locations much closer to the production office in Madrid. A forested area outside Segovia stood in for Valsain Wood, where Godfrey's Crusaders are ambushed. The Crusaders' encampment was also shot there. In Avila's great cathedral the production filmed the coronation scene.

The Moorish influence remains strongest in southern Spain; it was in and around Sevilla that locations were found for many of the interior scenes in Jerusalem. One of its most famous sites, the Alcazar, hosted the filming of several scenes in King Baldwin's palace. "We were very lucky to get permission to use the Alcazar, as well as the Casa di Pilatos, a 15th-century reproduction of of Pontius

Cast and extras in a scene filmed on the walls of Essaouira, Morocco, but meant to be Messina, the seaport in Sicily where Balian embarks for the Holy Land. Inset photo shows CG ships in the Messina harbor.

Pilate's residence in Jerusalem. We took advantage of its beautiful tiled courtyard in particular," says Max.

Just outside Sevilla was another important location: a villa in Palma del Rio that became Godfrey's (and later Balian's) town home in Jerusalem. It also served as the hospital in Messina–the Italian seaport from where many Crusader voyages departed. "Again, we were lucky," notes Max, "because they were about to strip this beautiful place for renovation, turn it into a tourist hotel."

Morocco offered the production many places to shoot. "The variety of locations is panoramic for a country about the size of California. You have mountain regions, deserts, semi-arid regions, and beautiful coastline on both the Atlantic and Mediterranean. There are forests and lakes. This can be a lot of different places. You've got a great deal of architectural history with cities like Fez, Marrakech, and Ouarzazate. I love the desert light, and the vistas here are very powerful."

Another advantage, Max points out, is that Morocco has a well-developed film industry: "They've been making films in Morocco for a long time." The hub of movie activity is Ouarzazate, a town at the foot of the Atlas Mountains that's also the gateway for tourism into the Sahara. Beginning with *Lawrence of Arabia*, many well-known movies have been made in the vicinity, including Scott's *Gladiator* and *Black Hawk Down*, as well as *Troy*, *Alexander*, and *Star Wars: Episode 1*. Atlas Studios, just outside town, provides soundstages, workshop space, and trained crews for these productions.

Scott and Max wanted to get off the beaten track of locations around Ouarzazate, so they spent days bouncing around the desert in an SUV. That's how Max came across the place that became Ibelin: a cluster of five tiny settlements built around an ancient caravansary or caravan stop. Its casbah was carefully reshaped by Max's crew for the set and later restored to its original condition.

About a kilometer away, on a wide-open plain, they found a suitable site to build *Kingdom*'s cen-

Above: The Castle of Loarre in northern Spain, and the village set under construction. Top right: The Berber Cave location in Morocco, with Arthur Max's notes about the scene to be filmed there ("Guy sees caravan.") Right: Cast and crew on the Ibelin set, near Ouarzazate.

terpiece set: the exterior of Jerusalem. A road had to be improved and set construction facilities installed in order to use the site, but it offered what they needed: a certain amount of privacy and a generous sweep of open space where Scott could stage his climactic siege before the city walls.

Max was somewhat concerned about re-creating Jerusalem in such a bleak desert environment, given that the real city was set in a landscape of hills, cypress trees, and gardens. He soon realized, though, that such landscape elements could be found elsewhere around Ouarzazate, or could be replicated by visual effects. One such place was the citadel of Ait Ben Haddou, where he and Scott had earlier built a major set for *Gladiator*. In *Kingdom* they used it for the infamous hill of Golgotha, where Balian experiences his deepest crisis of faith.

A new and versatile Moroccan location was

the port city of Essaouira, a one-time Portuguese fortress on the coast west of Marrakech. It offered places to shoot street scenes and certain interiors in "Jerusalem," and its harbor could stand in for the port of Messina. (Many shots in Messina as well as Jerusalem would cut back and forth between footage shot in two different countries.) Ships of Crusaders and traders would be added to the harbor scene through the magic of CGI.

By the time cameras rolled, most but not quite all the locations were set. One day well into the Morocco shoot, Max drove by a large "palmery," a palm orchard set amidst cultivated wheat fields. Something clicked in his head and he wanted a closer look. Scott had recently asked for a script change so that a scene featuring Sibylla would take place not inside the palace but in a little summerhouse.

"I had to park and walk a half hour to get in there," Max recalls, "but what I found was such a beautiful, peaceful green place. There was a tiny village where the tomb of a holy person was preserved; people went there to pray. I finally coaxed Ridley there when he had a rare day off. He loved it, and it became the summerhouse."

Talking in Pictures

Ridley Scott famously communicates with his staff through drawings. Quick and accurate with pen or pencil, he is liable to grab any handy scrap of paper—a script page, a call sheet—and sketch an idea that's just come to him for how something should look: from a perspective on a battle to an actor's reaction. While shooting in Morocco, Scott would diagram camera set-ups in the sand.

Others talk back to him in pictures as well. The conversation about any film starts with source material and "scrap" for inspiration. "It's a tear-sheet process," says Arthur Max. "We pin it all up on the wall and Ridley absorbs it. For the big set pieces, he will scribble his Ridleygrams while he's talking, little diagrams of his initial thoughts. Then we'll usually bring in a concept artist to develop grander, more detailed drawings that reflect a general approach—but we're still searching for ideas. On *Kingdom*, the overall concepts came together pretty quickly."

The next stage in production design is to create set drawings to scale. Scott reviews many of these massively detailed renderings himself, and in any case he has set the direction through work at the concept stage and remains in close touch with Max throughout.

Storyboarding is central to Scott's journey from the screenplay to the screen. From his first reading of a draft script, he is making pictures in his head and often scribbling on the script pages. He is unequivocal about the importance of storyboarding: "If you can board, you should.

"Storyboarding is critical to all the movies I've done," Scott declares. "It's the best way to get ideas across to everyone from studio

***Left:* Concept drawing of the Jerusalem set by Pier Luigi Basile.**
***Above:* Concept illustration of Saladin's tent by Rob Cowper.**

heads to the production team. You are literally working out what you can do." He learned the economic value of storyboards while *Alien* was in the planning stage: the budget was doubled after he presented his storyboards.

"I might use very rough drawings as a guide for the more fully executed version. Often I'm doing these in the back of a car, or while reading the script or in a meeting." Scott carries around three gray felt-tip pens at all times, with tip widths from fine to broad. "They allow me very quickly to create a variety of tones and washes that give the storyboard much more atmosphere and depth."

Because of the pressures on his time, Scott sometimes works with a storyboard artist but finds it somewhat frustrating. "It can take more time to explain what I want to the artist than it would to do it myself. Unless they are really good." In *Kingdom of Heaven*, parts of the big action sequences were farmed out to other artists and those drawings "edited" by Scott as needed. When film editor Dody Dorn saw all the storyboards together, she could tell instantly which were Scott's. "Not only is his style so distinctive, but they convey emotion in just a few pencil strokes."

After the shoot begins, Scott's drawings continue to make their way through the crew: a new board showing how a shot will change, a detail he wants to make sure doesn't get missed. Keeping track of these ephemeral documents is a challenge. "We're always trying to keep Ridley's input in one place," notes Max, "but sometimes I'd have to chase down the person whose call sheet or script he had just scribbled on."

The visual conversation extends all the way through post-production. As the visual effects team generates composited "plates" that incorporate their enhancements, those images come to Scott. He in turn draws on them—adding a detail, adjusting the lighting, shifting the view within the frame—and sends them back to the VFX artists for further work.

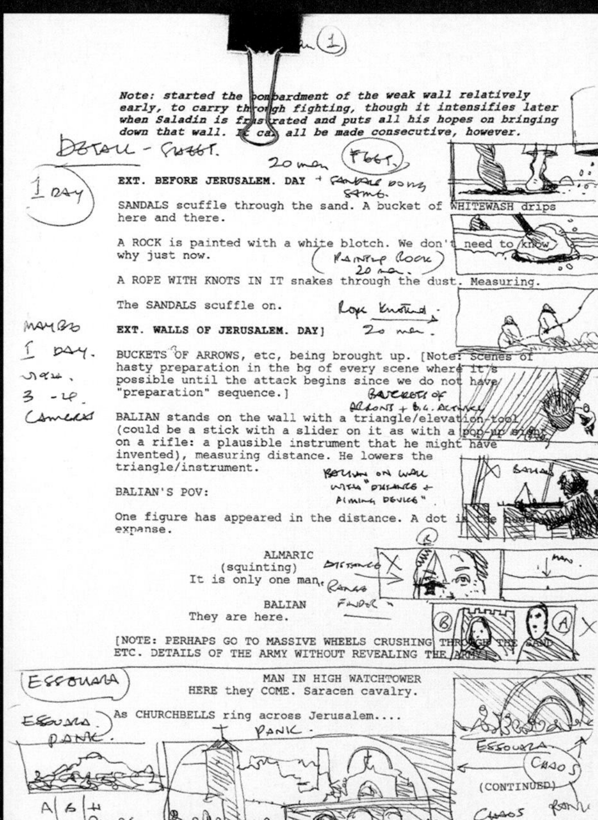

Note: started the bombardment of the weak wall relatively early, to carry through fighting, though it intensifies later when Saladin is frustrated and puts all his hopes on bringing down that wall. It can all be made consecutive, however.

EXT. BEFORE JERUSALEM. DAY

SANDALS scuffle through the sand. A bucket of WHITEWASH drips here and there.

A ROCK is painted with a white blotch. We don't need to know why just now.

A ROPE WITH KNOTS IN IT snakes through the dust. Measuring.

The SANDALS scuffle on.

EXT. WALLS OF JERUSALEM. DAY]

BUCKETS OF ARROWS, etc, being brought up. [Note: Scenes of hasty preparation in the bg of every scene where it's possible until the attack begins since we do not have "preparation" sequence.]

BALIAN stands on the wall with a triangle/elevation-tool (could be a stick with a slider on it as with a pop-up sight on a rifle: a plausible instrument that he might have invented), measuring distance. He lowers the triangle/instrument.

BALIAN'S POV:

One figure has appeared in the distance. A dot in the huge expanse.

ALMARIC
(squinting)
It is only one man.

BALIAN
They are here.

[NOTE: PERHAPS GO TO MASSIVE WHEELS CRUSHING THROUGH THE SAND ETC. DETAILS OF THE ARMY WITHOUT REVEALING THE ARMY.]

MAN IN HIGH WATCHTOWER
HERE they COME. Saracen cavalry.

As CHURCHBELLS ring across Jerusalem....

(CONTINUED)

***Top:** A VFX "plate" on which Scott has drawn. **Center:** A "Ridleygram." **Right:** Annotated page from one of Scott's scripts.*

The following samples of Scott's storyboards may not reflect the final edited film seen in theaters. As the story opens, a pair of grave-diggers are burying a young woman—a suicide—at a cross-roads in the bitter cold of a French winter.

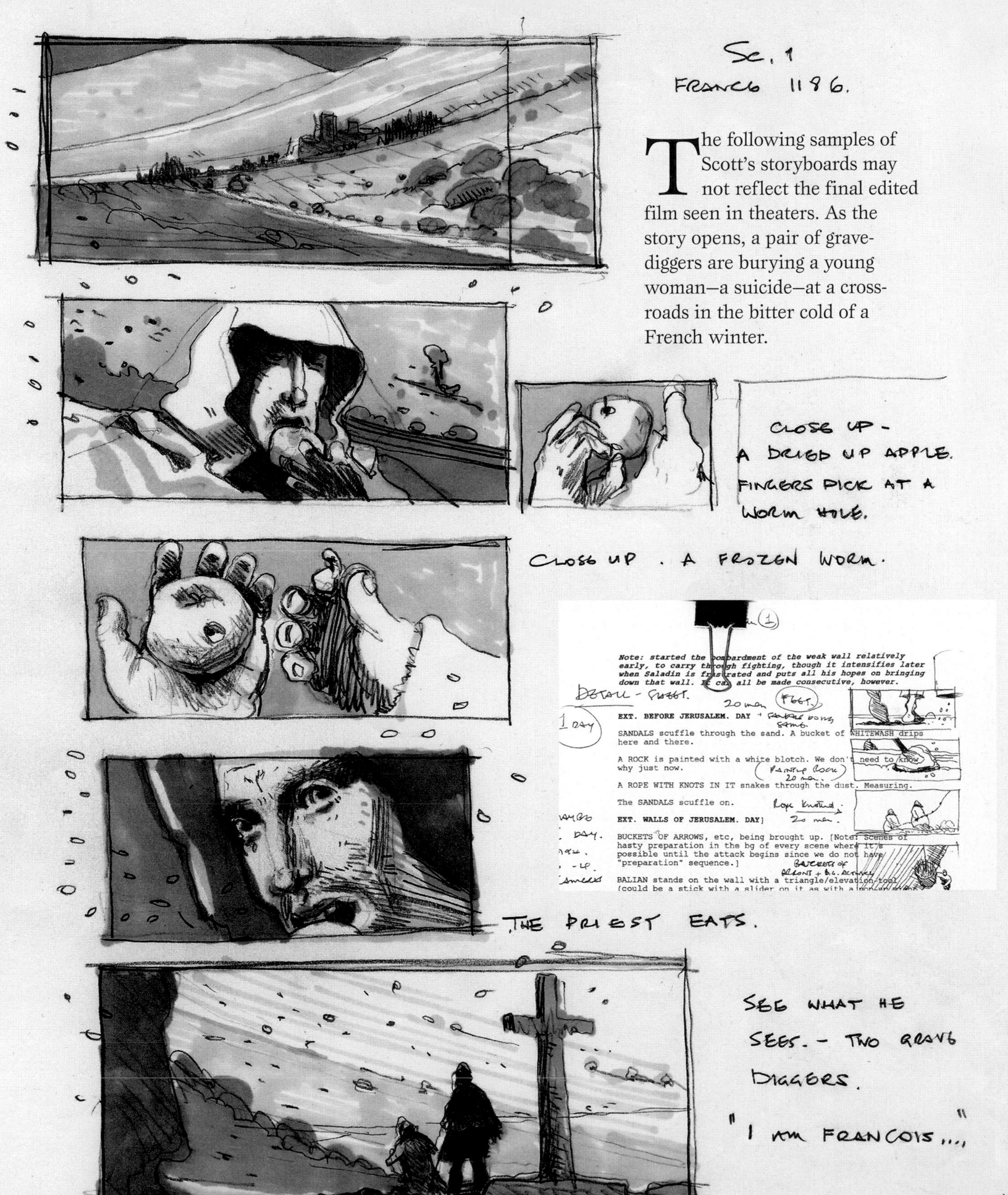

Note: started the bombardment of the weak wall relatively early, to carry through fighting, though it intensifies later when Saladin is frustrated and puts all his hopes on bringing down that wall. It can all be made consecutive, however.

EXT. BEFORE JERUSALEM. DAY

SANDALS scuffle through the sand. A bucket of WHITEWASH drips here and there.

A ROCK is painted with a white blotch. We don't need to know why just now.

A ROPE WITH KNOTS IN IT snakes through the dust. Measuring.

The SANDALS scuffle on.

EXT. WALLS OF JERUSALEM. DAY]

BUCKETS OF ARROWS, etc, being brought up. [Note: Scenes of hasty preparation in the bg of every scene where it's possible until the attack begins since we do not have "preparation" sequence.]

BALIAN stands on the wall with a triangle/elevation-tool (could be a stick with a slider on it as with a

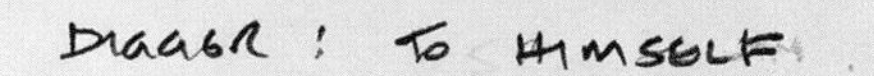

" I AM FRANCOIS, TO MY DISMAY

OVER THE OTHERS TOILING BACK... WE SEE A SHROUDED BODY.

THE WIND BLOWS REVEALING THE FACE OF A YOUNG WOMAN

AS THE PRIEST COMES FORWARD

AND STANDS OVER THE BODY.....EYEING THE CROSS AROUND HER NECK.

An unscrupulous priest supervises this burial in unhallowed ground. As he steals a cross from the woman's neck, the work is interrupted by a party of knights returning from the Crusades. They are led by Godfrey of Ibelin, whose family lands lie nearby.

WALKS TO HIS FORGE

BALIAN: TO BOY.

"WE SHALL GO TO WORK."

SC10.

WE WORK

MONTAGE

FIRE, IRON, WATER.

SC10.

"YOU ARE THE BLACKSMITH?

"REMAIN"!

EXT. FORGE

ARRIVAL OF GODFREY + GROUP.

During his brief visit home, Godfrey seeks out the young blacksmith at his forge. He has information to impart about events that took place long before, when Balian's father was blacksmith on the estate—news that will change both their lives.

GODFREY.

The priest, Balian's brother, wishes him gone and has long urged him to seek his fortune by crusading. It doesn't interest Balian—until the priest taunts him with a vision of his dead wife in hell, driving Balian to kill him.

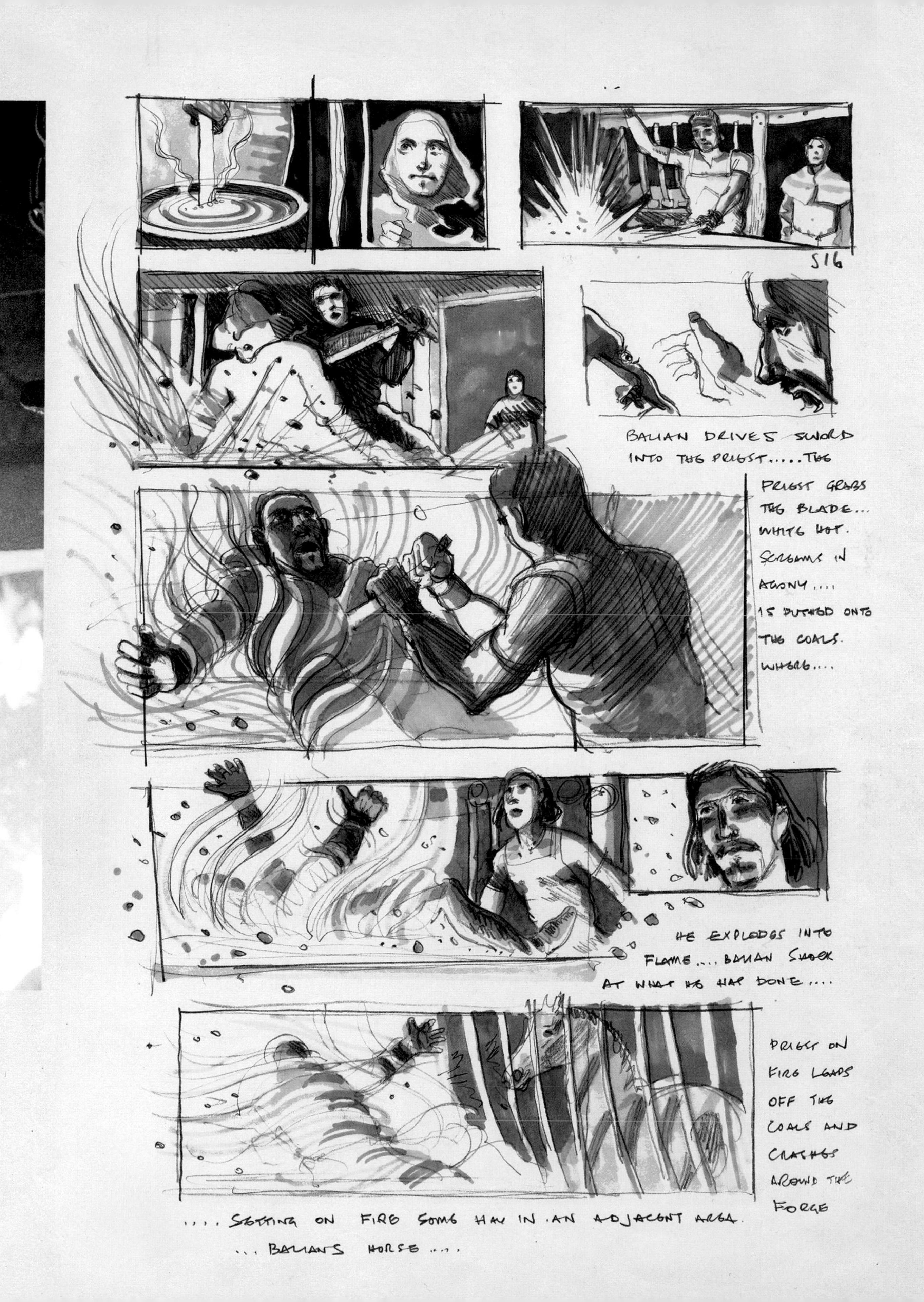
516
BALIAN DRIVES SWORD INTO THE PRIEST.....THE
PRIEST GRABS THE BLADE... WHITE HOT. SCREAMS IN AGONY.... IS PUSHED ONTO THE COALS. WHERE....
HE EXPLODES INTO FLAME.... BALIAN SHOCK AT WHAT HE HAS DONE....
PRIEST ON FIRE LEAPS OFF THE COALS AND CRASHES AROUND THE FORGE
.... SETTING ON FIRE SOME HAY IN AN ADJACENT AREA. ... BALIANS HORSE ....

Having fled France and joined Godfrey's Crusaders, Balian makes his long and perilous journey to the Holy Land, hoping to redeem his sins and his wife's soul. But even on the the holy hill of Golgotha, where Christ was said to be crucified, he finds no salvation. As other pilgrims make their way up the hillside, he buries her cross there.

Burying the Cross.

windy
Dust

windy
Dust.

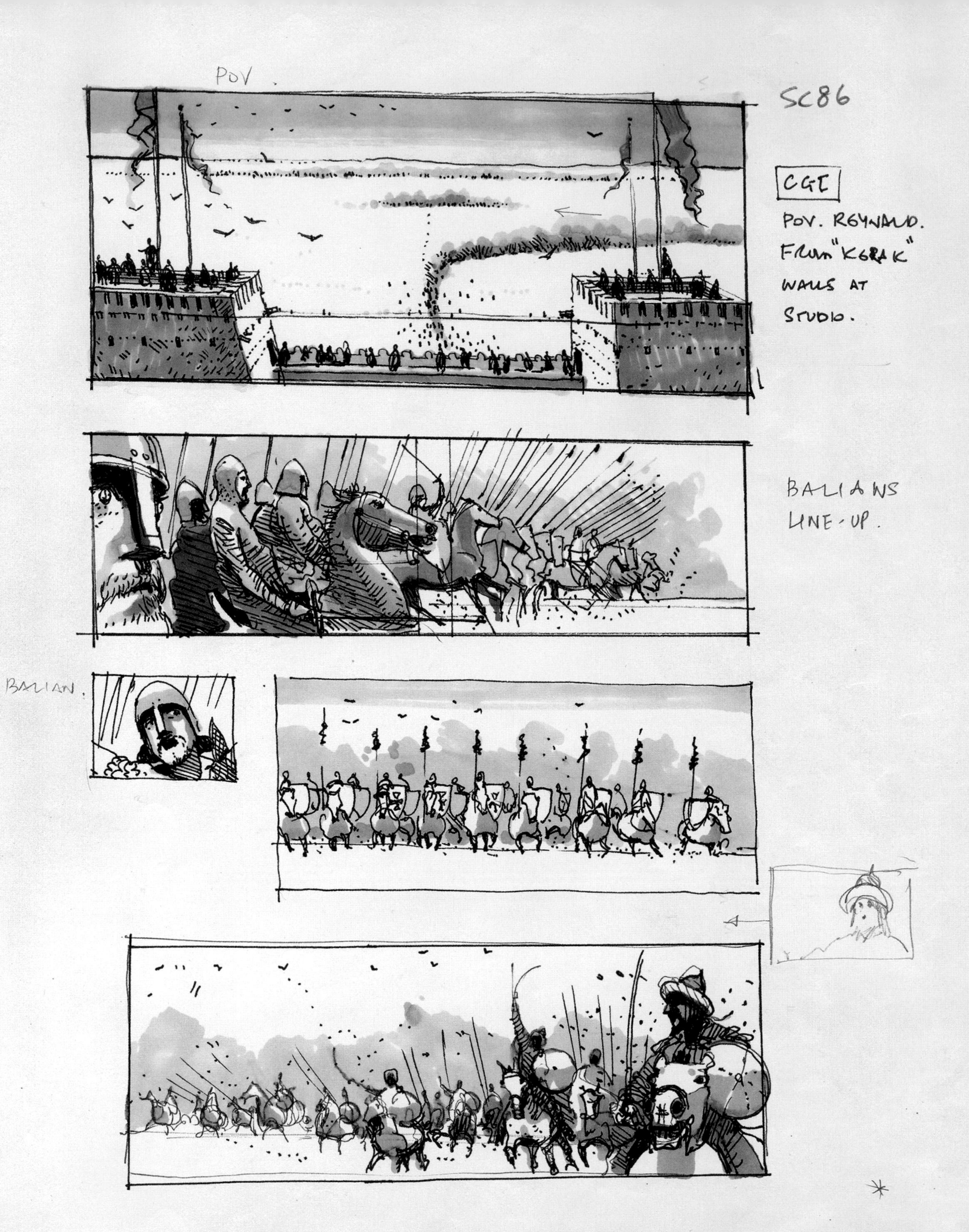
POV
SC86
CGI
POV. REYNALD.
FROM "KERAK"
WALLS AT
STUDIO.
BALIANS
LINE-UP.
BALIAN.

The King of Jerusalem, whom Balian is sworn to serve, leads his men to the frontier castle of Kerak, where the outlaw baron Reynald is barricaded against Saladin's forces. Before the king arrives, Balian leads his Ibelin knights to the defense of villagers seeking refuge in the castle. Reynald and the princess Sibylla watch from the battlements.

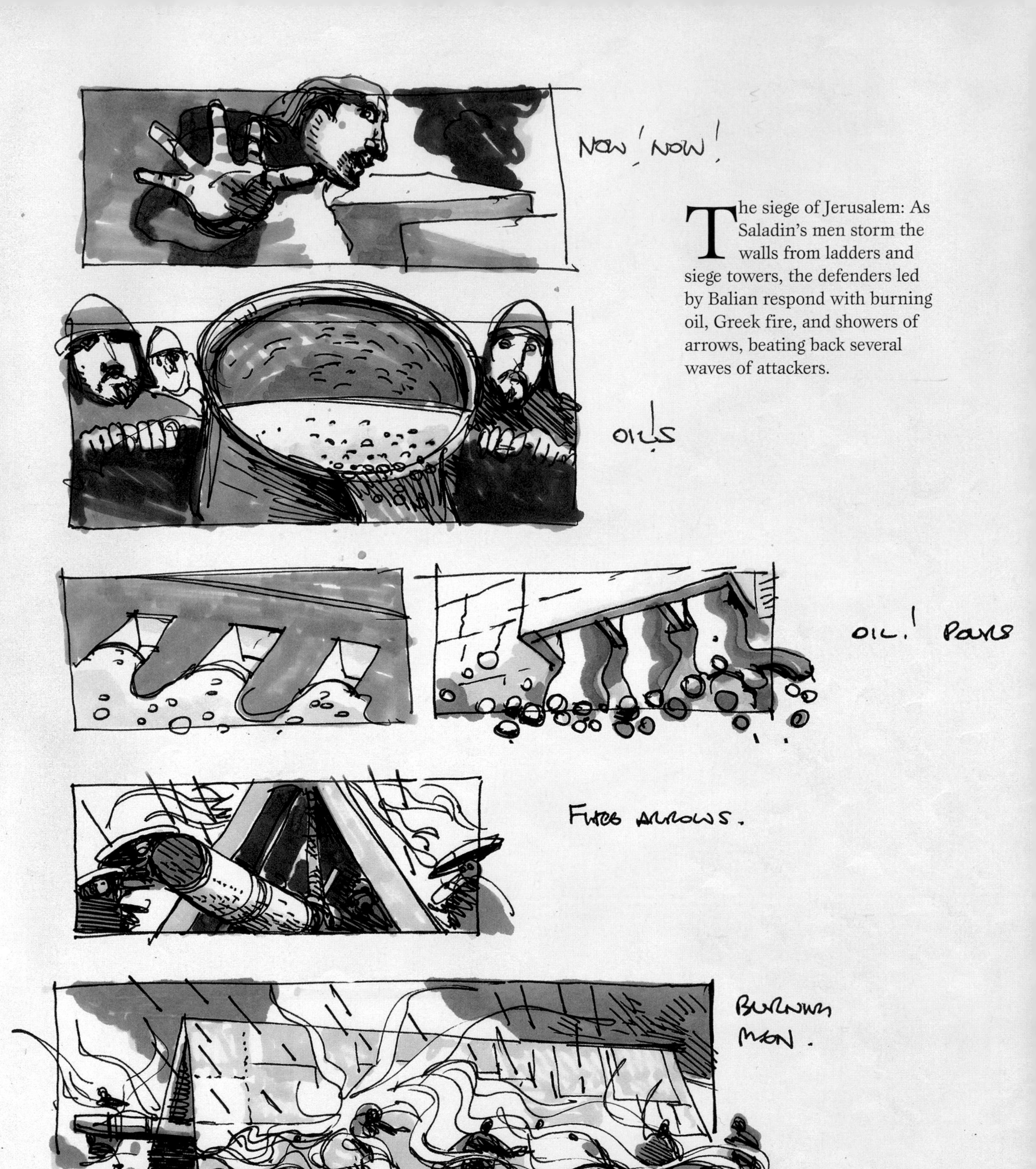

The siege of Jerusalem: As Saladin's men storm the walls from ladders and siege towers, the defenders led by Balian respond with burning oil, Greek fire, and showers of arrows, beating back several waves of attackers.

Sets for All Seasons

In creating sets Ridley Scott and Max set the bar high for themselves and their crew, regardless of time pressures. "We had a very compressed period of preparation for the construction, so we were still designing as we were building," Max admits. "And the range of imagery was very wide, from simple village life to the opulence of the king's palace in Jerusalem."

The process began with research, concept drawings, and location scouting, as detailed in earlier chapters. At the same time, Max was assembling staff for several art departments, which would build models, draw up detailed set blueprints, and then execute the construction on location.

"We had several art departments in different places," notes Max. "One worked mainly on the sets for Spain, under supervising art director John King. They started out in London and then moved to Madrid. The larger group, working on the big sets for Morocco, was based at Cinecittà in Rome—they are mostly Italian, with a world of experience in doing these epic-scale sets." This team, under supervising art director Marco Trentini, produced drawings for sets and set decoration while beginning to set up facilities in Morocco.

"The Moroccan department actually started ahead of the Spanish group even though they were

***Left:** Elevation drawing for the palace wall in the Jerusalem set by Roberta Federico.*

Follow the Sun

One of the most challenging aspects of building a set this size of Jerusalem was knowing how to position it in relation to where the sun would be several months later, when the director was trying to light his shots naturally.

Before staking out the set, Arthur Max's team researched the sun's projected azimuth in the spring of 2004 and took readings with a GPS compass on the site. This information was sent to a visual effects expert in 3D modeling, who came up with a quick set model using Lightwave software. The model showed various angles at which the sun would strike the set surfaces at different days and different times of day over the nine-week shoot.

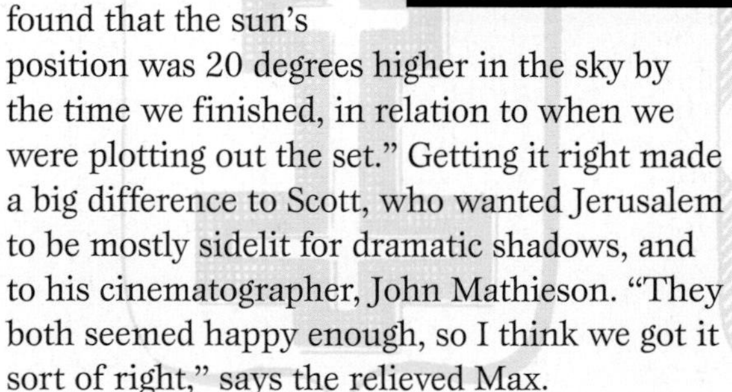

"It was early spring when we started shooting in Morocco, and June when we finished," says Max. "I think we found that the sun's position was 20 degrees higher in the sky by the time we finished, in relation to when we were plotting out the set." Getting it right made a big difference to Scott, who wanted Jerusalem to be mostly sidelit for dramatic shadows, and to his cinematographer, John Mathieson. "They both seemed happy enough, so I think we got it sort of right," says the relieved Max.

shooting later, because they had a bigger nut to crack," says Max. When the drawing phase was done, after about six weeks, some of them moved on to Ouarzazate. "At one point we actually had three art departments functioning like an assembly line in three countries."

Other early steps included preparing sites for the larger sets—sometimes building or improving roads—and conducting light-angle studies of the sites (see sidebar). Before doing detailed renderings of the big sets (Jerusalem, Ibelin, Balian's village), Max's team "previsualized" them in computer models. Eventual set construction was documented in photos to assist with later VFX work.

Set construction proper began in late September 2003 and went on for about 20 weeks. The entire Jerusalem set was staked out by mid-October. Both principal locations were home to large international crews, especially in Morocco, where crews included Italian, Spanish, Croatian, English, and of course Moroccan workers. This crew numbered around 350 at the height of construction, the team in Spain around 150—in addition to art departments totalling around 100, including set decorators and prop staff.

"It was one of the largest art departments I've ever been involved with," says Max, "and the confusion factor was high because of the number of countries and languages we were dealing with. But everyone handled it well, and that complexity is an enjoyable part of these large-scale projects. Everyone brings something different to the table, and I think the mixture of cultures is healthy."

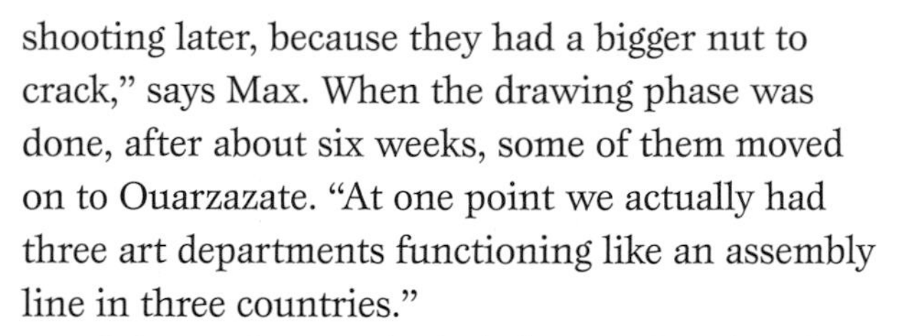

LEFT: Light studies of the Jerusalem set, March 1, 2004. TOP RIGHT: The art department "bullpen" in Ouarzazate with art directors Gianni Giovagnoni, Antonio Tarolla, and Monica Sallustio. RIGHT: Arthur Max in front of the Kerak set.

For Max as well as Scott, the payoff is worth the enormous effort. "Exercising our passion for historical accuracy is a game that we all like to play," says Max, "and combining research with imagination to create these deeply textured worlds. The actors get a better feel for the period if they can meander through an environment where life is taking place on lots of different levels. The set should be a living place."

Balian's France

Scott establishes the medieval time frame with opening sequences in a feudal village in France, where Balian springs from. The castle of the local lord (Godfrey's brother) came with the location at Loarre in the Spanish Pyrénées. Its surrounding walls and gates needed renovation, and the production built platforms and staircases to provide access for actors and extras. They also added a splendid 22-foot-high fireplace in the main hall—and of course the rooms had to be dressed for shooting. But otherwise the fine old castle offered all they needed.

The village, though, had to be built from scratch—and to make it look and feel as authentic as possible Max was determined to rely on techniques and materials similar to what would have been used in 1187 A.D. He researched the rural vernacular buildings of that era through books and networks of period enthusiasts such as England's Society for the Preservation of Ancient Monuments. And he sought to learn where those techniques were still being used in Europe.

He found them not far away, in the northwestern Spanish region of Galicia. "There were still

craftsmen there who did slate roofs, thatching, and stone drywalling. We brought about a dozen of them in to our location, and their work enabled us to be pretty on the nose for the period."

Real timbers, thatch, slate, and stone were used to create several small dwellings, a medieval granary (which concealed an existing coffee shop and some kids' play equipment on the site), and of course Balian's forge. Other construction was done by able craftsmen from Spain's film industry, such as the roof of a church that is under construction in the story (the local bishop needs Balian's skills to finish it). The interior of the forge building with its huge, blackened beams was also created on the Loarre site.

Building open-air sets in the mountain winter brought its difficulties. Says Max, "We were flooded out several times by storms, and had to rebuild part of our set." The village was sited in a flat area where water collected, so heavy equipment sometimes got stuck. And at least some of the snow that fell on the set was real.

The Holy Land: Ibelín

Surprisingly to them, the crews building sets in Morocco had to contend with the elements too. Winter rains and wind assailed the locations after three consecutive drought years. "We were trying to do plaster and paint in driving horizontal rain—which seems ironic given that this is supposed to be a desert," Max comments.

Kingdom of Heaven's two largest sets were located about an hour apart in the valley outside Ouarzazate. The Jerusalem set was entirely free-standing, built from the ground up. But the set for Ibelin, the estate where Balian makes his home in the Holy Land, was an imaginative elaboration on existing structures.

Max found the spot—a small complex of old villages along a major *wadi*, or riverbed—by "just nosing around this region we already knew." It resonated for him with a description in the screenplay, and the production arranged permission to build onto the local "casbah" or fortified house, which was about five centuries old. "The place was so

charming because it's relatively untouched. There's not a lot of electricity—it's a kind of time warp."

Many of the old casbah were caravansarai, Max explains: places where caravans could rest and find water on their route through the Atlas Mountains, as well as safe shelter overnight for people and animals. Over hundreds of years, villagers would continue to repair and add to these mud buildings.

"This type of architecture was generic to the Holy Land, and the design of these buildings would have been in use during the correct period for our story," notes Max. Modeling details on the original casbah, the production team added the structures of Balian's Ibelin—a fortified gate, watchtowers, a two-story villa, a courtyard, stables,

Above: Views of the extensive Ibelin set under construction.
Left: A composed frame from the film shows the "France" set including the village, Balian's forge and Loarre Castle.

and a biblical-style well. The style is similar to the local buildings, but richer.

As with the French village, they used traditional techniques and materials almost entirely. "It was really a learning curve for me—normally we're working with modern materials to make things lightweight and quick to move," says Max. "Here we threw away our film technology and built in a traditional way, using stone and mud and posts made from real palm trees instead of store-bought lumber." Local craftsmen and workers from Fez helped build and decorate the set with their traditional motifs, so that it would match the existing casbah as closely as possible. They also made bricks and hand-fired thousands of tiles in their kilns for roofs and floors.

"We really wanted to get the textures and the organic feel of the landscape," Max adds. "It was a pleasure to watch these local craftsmen express themselves when given the opportunity, because normally they don't have the money to build like this."

Agriculture was integral to this part of the story, as Balian works with his Ibelin people to irrigate fields and grow crops in once-barren land. After the "barren field" shots had been done, villagers were asked to start cultivating land in the riverbed. About half the plants seen in the film were grown in the field and the rest brought in by greensmen. Nearly the entire population of village complex were employed as extras at this stage, digging actual wells and irrigation channels.

Building in "lived-in" locations had its challenges as well as rewards; the production needed to work around the residents. Official permission was obtained for all this activity, including water diversion. Says Max, "What we try to do is incorporate the local community as much as possible, make them feel involved. Having them work on the actual fabrication of the sets is a good way to do it."

The Two-Faced Set

Vast, stark, and solitary, an amazing structure arose from the desolate Draa Valley, a high plateau just below the Atlas Mountains. Ridley Scott's re-creation of medieval Jerusalem during the reign of the Latin kings resembles the historical city in broad outline, with Scott's own dramatic flourishes.

"In our research we looked at all the fortified Crusader castles of that period in the Middle East,"

RIGHT: Filming siege action on the Jerusalem set. INSET: The Kerak main gate on the reverse side of Jerusalem. OVERLEAF: Concept drawing of the siege by Pier Luigi Basile. INSET: Ridley Scott uses a model of the Jerusalem/Kerak set and beat cards (in background) to map out the action.

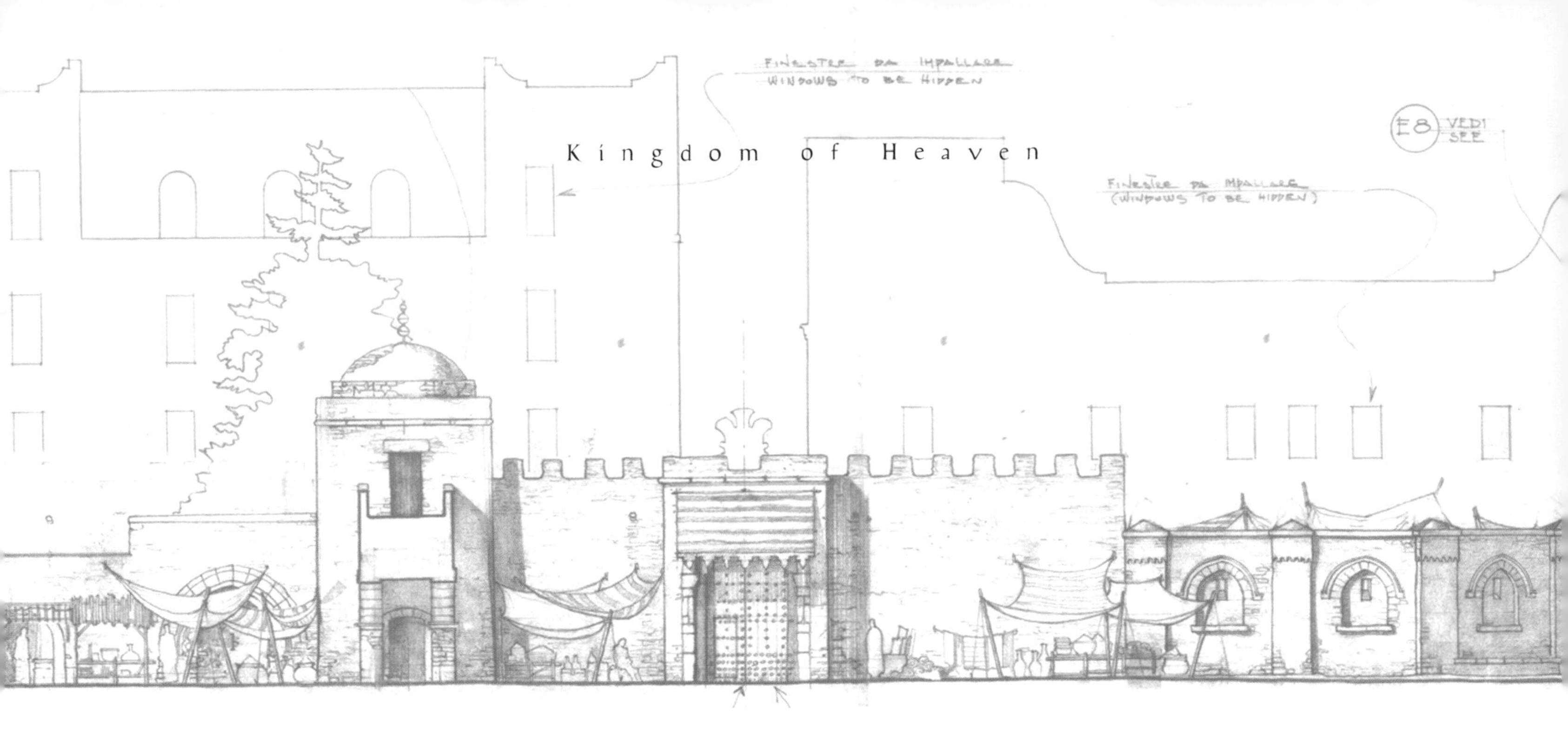

says Max. "We looked at the famous Krak de Chevaliers, the Hospitaler castle in Syria; we looked at Kerak, and of course at Jerusalem itself. Our set is a kind of amalgam of those images. Our city walls are modeled most directly after the Citadel area, the military heart of medieval Jerusalem, which has the Tower of David and David's Gate."

Approached from the south, the façade of the set stretches 575 feet across the valley on a slight rise–the Jerusalem side of the set, that is. For this is actually two sets in one, the opposite side representing the castle of Kerak. This Crusader outpost was the domain of Reynald of Chatillon and the site of a showdown between Saladin's army and King Baldwin's forces midway through the film story.

This "two-faced" set arose through a blend of cost contingencies and the director's imagination. At a critical stage of whittling down the film's budget to a workable level, Scott met with his executive producers and challenged them to find a breakthrough. Then it occurred to him: "Why do we have to have a castle for Kerak and the whole Jerusalem set. Why can't we use one side of Jerusalem to double as Kerak?" They did the math and realized that between construction costs and travel between sets, they could save around $5 million.

Scott made this solution work to the film's advantage, giving each set much greater depth and dimension by putting them back to back. Max explains how it works: "The two sets are grafted together, sharing a main tower and a large archway. When you're in the courtyard of the Kerak set, looking through the main arch, you're actually

Above: Elevation drawing of "David's Street" in the Jerusalem set. Below: Set model with soldiers and siege equipment.

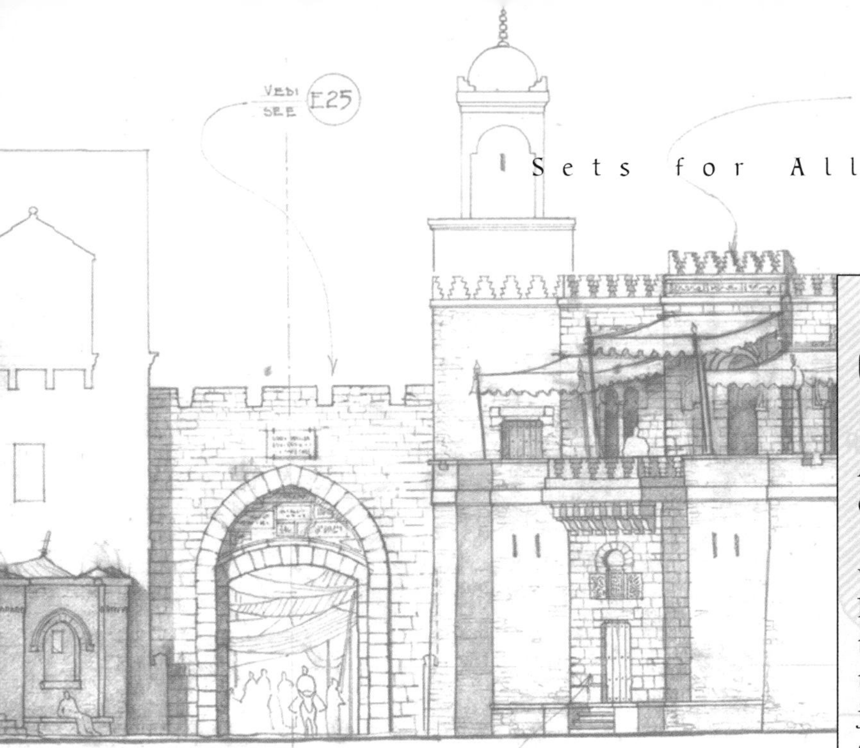

looking into the Jerusalem set, but disguised with set decoration and extras to look like an extension of Kerak. And vice versa from the Jerusalem side. On film you'll see much more detail above that's been added with CGI. But from ground level you get a true impression of depth, of space lit by natural daylight and filled with dust or smoke, which lends much more realism than a green-screen effect."

Kerak, actually in present-day Jordan some 50 miles southwest of Jerusalem, is a ruin today. The set design was based on the Aleppo Citadel in Syria, built in the 10th century, and the mountain-top Crusader castle of Calatrava in Spain. "The idea was that this same real estate had been fought over many times," notes Max. Fragments of Kerak were built on the set—the main gate and courtyard, partial walls, a balcony—and much else filled in by VFX later, using plates of old architectural details shot in several Morocco cities.

The confrontation between Balian and Saladin's cavalry before Kerak was actually shot in the next valley over from the set, a wide, flat plain. Visual effects make it look as though the castle towers above the battlefield on a hilltop. Actors

The Jerusalem Puzzle

The film's Jerusalem was an amalgam of found locations, built set pieces, and CGI effects—to such an extent, says Arthur Max, that probably only Ridley Scott could keep it all straight in his head.

The exterior walls and some interior streets were built at the Ouarzazate set. A whole other layer of the city was created as a set in Essaouira, the historic Moroccan port town, incorporating the town's existing old walls. (Workers were just beginning to restore the walls, but Max persuaded officials to stop the work so they could be filmed in their beautifully aged state.) The production commandeered a major crossroads and built a set representing inner Jerusalem near the precincts of the palace. Also contained within this set are the entrance to Godfrey's town house, and Sibylla's balcony.

But it gets more complicated. Certain places in "Jerusalem" were actually locations in Spain, where action was filmed or views photographed. The palace is actually the Alcazar in Sevilla. Most of Balian's house and its lovely courtyard are a villa in Palma del Rio. In a parking lot outside that site, walls were built to match those in the Ouarzazate and Essaouira sets. Jerusalem's cathedral, seen in wide shots, is actually Avila Cathedral in Spain. And so on.

Audiences are unlikely to realize that a single shot may dart dizzyingly around the Mediterranean. For example: Sibylla invites Balian to her room (in the Alcazar). On the way there they pass through corridors from the Essaouira set. They exit to the balcony for a glimpse of Jerusalem at night (Ouarzazate set), then come back inside to yet another room in the Alcazar. "Ridley's great at getting the most from every set," Max confirms.

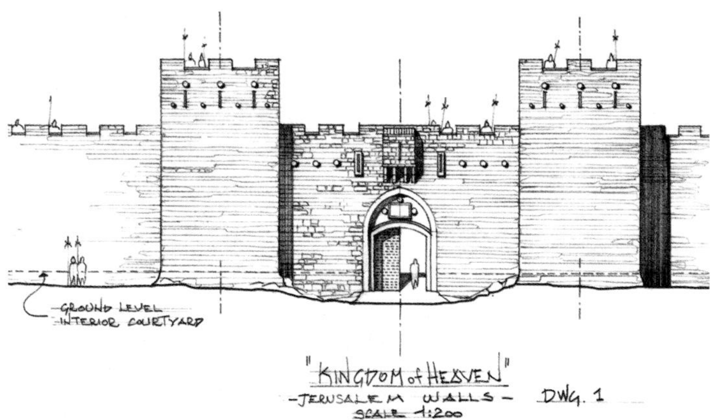

observing the clash from a balcony above were filmed on the set and then composited into the larger scene.

The entire set formed a huge rectangle oriented roughly east-west on its long axis. The Jerusalem (south) wall thus received sunlight for much of each day—this was important because it could take nearly all day to set up the big "beauty shots" done there. On the Kerak (north) side, Scott wanted to shoot Baldwin's entrance into the fortress with backlighting, so that was done in the morning.

The Jerusalem walls were 35 feet high, punctuated by towers that reached 48 to 54 feet. Within the fortified walls (which would be extended through VFX), the built set featured a dense urban environment that included tower rooms and balconies, four courtyards, armories, gates and arches, corridors, shops and café interiors, a camel market, and wine-warehouse district. Perspectives of market scenes could be glimpsed through every archway. Orlando Bloom, who had worked on the massive *Lord of the Rings* project, told Max it was the first time he had experienced a set as a complete environment.

ABOVE and BELOW: The Jerusalem set during construction. CENTER: Elevation drawing of Jerusalem walls and David's Gate by Alexandro Santucci.

Other pieces of Jerusalem were actually created in the city of Essaouira (see sidebar on page 131). From the old walls of that city, too, came patterns for the exterior stonework, which was all cast in plaster. "Essaouira has a lot of beautifully textured stone walls." notes Max.

As usual, making a set on this scale started with design models. "We brought them all onto the barren site here before we even began to build," says Max, "and tore bits away in the process of determining what was essential to the scenes we would be shooting." Then came the drawing phase—more than a thousand drawings were generated for just this set by 20 different artists.

Construction sheds were erected on the site for craftspeople who translated drawings into solid form. Molds for various set elements were fabricated in the Atlas workshops, then shipped to the set, where elements were cast and set in place.

Max points to the particular expertise his Italian crew brought to the undertaking. "A lot of the construction crew, particularly the Italians, come from a tradition of doing epic films as far back as *Ben-Hur* and *Cleopatra*. Many of them grew up working on those 'plaster-and-paint' sets, doing elaborate molding, casting and finishing—and brought all their skill accumulated over 35 years to this film."

For the scale of the build, he suggests, the closest comparison might be the famous Circus Maximus set of *Ben-Hur.* "Quite a few people involved with this project worked on that set, which they say took about six months to build. And this set, on about the same scale, took five months. Considering that it's almost 40 years later, and the costs of labor and materials have grown so much, it's very ambitious of the studio to take on a set build of this size."

Dressing the Sets

Inside the walls of any period set goes a mind-boggling array of things, from a humble cooking pot in a peasant's hut to the lavish hangings of a palace. Not to mention all the props that get carried on the backs of horses, in the hands of flag bearers, or in vehicles. All this is the realm of the set decorator; on *Kingdom* a young Englishwoman named Sonja Klaus.

"For a set decorator a film like this is a dream," says Klaus. "It's not like doing a modern-day piece in a middle-class London suburb. It's twelfth century, and everything has to be made from scratch. It gives one chance to do a huge amount of manufacturing. So when Arthur said 'It's the Crusades,' I thought I'd died and gone to heaven."

Max understands the challenge. "So many things on this type of project have to be manufactured. Twelfth-century ceramics, for example, are not readily available. But in both Spain and Morocco, the ceramic and metalwork and leather-

ABOVE: Set decorator Sonja Klaus shopping for props in Morocco.

"Ridley Scott Likes a Flag"

Arthur Max's observation is surely an understatement, since *Kingdom of Heaven* may be the biggest movie showcase ever for flags and banners. Some 650 different designs are featured; some true to historical models and others designed for the film.

Medieval flag motifs were clear signs of rank, as well as helping combatants identify friends and foe in battle. Every military order had its flag, of course, as did every lord with his vassal knights, and different groups of soldiers loyal to the king. On the Muslim side, various troops within Saladin's forces had their own distinctive designs.

Set decorator Sonja Klaus commissioned flags to be manufactured for the film in Spain, England, India, and Morocco. Those associated with important characters were often of superb quality. Note Klaus, "A lot of the posh flags have beautiful stitching done in India—they do the most wonderful work there with metallic thread. We also had a lot of beautiful hand stitching done in England, as well as silk screening, and appliqué work."

working industries are still alive and well. We used a lot of local craftsmanship."

Klaus did her research in many of the same sources used by Max. "I got inspiration from the Orientalists and George de La Tour—his moody paintings have wonderful light in them. The Orientalists for the splendor and scale, the locations and textures. And the paintings in the Salle de Croisades we used especially for flags, banners, and horse dressing.

"When you start a film and you're working out how many props you need to make or rent, you first break down the script. Certain things you know you must have, like all the action props, because they are in the script. Then you go by the situations—is there a bedroom, a stable, a dining room? And add various touches you may have found in the reference, for example, the camel dressing."

Where possible Klaus tried to use colors that related to the period, but she didn't have to restrict her palette by exact historical fidelity. The Orientalist art suggested more intense color, which she knew would be to Scott's liking. "A very bright blue might make you think, oh, they'd never have had that then. But if it works, it's right."

After a show-and-tell session with Scott to establish directions, she put together a book of samples for costume designer Janty Yates. Yates provided feedback, and Klaus would frequently check with her before making choices—for example, how an actor was costumed for scene might guide what kind of fabric she'd put on a couch.

To run her departments and manage props, Klaus had a staff of 45 experienced crew from England and around Europe, as well as local labor

OPPOSITE: Jeremy Irons as Tiberias and one of the palace interiors in Seville.

at each production office or set. "At one point I know we had about 120 people." Storeman Chas Jellis was on the front lines in tracking, warehousing, and distributing the thousands of props among the dressing prop men, who placed the items in the sets. And there was a team of expert craftspeople for every task: from drapes and dyeing, to leather and painting, to modelmaking, woodwork, and metalwork. Draftsmen created renderings for furnishings to be manufactured. Klaus's personal favorite was the "bamboo man. He would sit at the back in a little shack all day long and make wonderful things out of bamboo and wicker–animal cages, frames for the howdahs."

Some aspects of her dream assignment were less dreamy than others. "Shooting in Spain was logistically a nightmare," she says, because the Loarre set and the southern Spain locations were so distant from the production office and manufacturing facilities in Madrid. Some of the hired locations caused headaches. "A designed location is easier because you can punch holes in the wall if you have to. Working in a hired location like the Alcazar, you have to be very sensitive to what's there."

Klaus has nothing but praise, though, for her bosses on the film. "Arthur is a really brilliant designer. I like working with him because he lets me do my own thing quite a lot of the time.

"And it's incredible to work with someone like Ridley, because he loves everything we do. I knew that if I spent hours manufacturing a prop or buying really exquisite fabric, and I showed it to him, it would be in the film. No doubt. And he loves fabrics; he'll dress the set himself if you're not there. So none of the fatigue and tears and anxiety are wasted, because it will be on that screen."

The extraordinary care taken in dressing his sets was part of Scott's process of re-creating a period. "The atmosphere is deepened by incorporating countless small objects that people don't think about, that speak to how people cook their meals or carry their water," says Max. "It all gives a kind of density to the dream."

Above: Dining hall of Godfrey's family castle, filmed in Loarre, Spain. Opposite: Extending the illusion: Jerusalem before (left) and after CGI effects.

Blurring the Lines

Creating the worlds seen in *Kingdom of Heaven* is an organic process that starts in Ridley Scott's imagination and proceeds through many stages. "Things evolve throughout the production but it all goes back to his initial conceptions," notes Max, "his desire to achieve monumental scale in these fortresses. The actual set pieces, big as they were, are relatively puny compared to the final result."

Where the artistry comes in, Max believes is in "blurring the lines–that is, confusing the issue of what's real or existing with what's been added on. Making the edges unclear so you can't really tell what we've done, what was there before, and what's been generated in a computer afterwards."

This applies in a physical sense to the Ibelin set, where structural designs were integrated with ancient materials. It involves set dressing, camera angles, and lighting, as in making the Jerusalem and Kerak sets blend together to enlarge each. And of course it is deeply woven with the VFX work used to extend sets and add detail.

Knowing the extent to which CGI will be used is vital to the production designer's decision making, says Max. "It affects how to use your resources and how the director will shoot the sequences. How much live-action coverage there is. What amount of building you need to do to cover those sequences, and where the impact of a very wide angle shot with large amounts of CGI will be most advantageous. Which locations serve best.

"Our approach is a balance: we do the minimum amount of building needed to make it convincing to today's rather sophisticated audiences, who can spot an all-CGI movie. We start off with the real elements, generated from a real location, do a certain amount of construction, and then extend from there. Again, the aim is to deceive the eye a bit, to blur the edges.

"If we've done the job well–and I don't think anyone is better at it than Ridley–it's all seamless, the design and effects are imperceptible, and you can't really see the edges.

"It's inspirational to work with a director like Ridley Scott. The projects that he sets for himself are always challenging. He raises the bar in contemporary filmmaking all the time, both technically–in the standards he sets for all the departments–and emotionally, in the way he likes to tell stories."

TIBERIAS.
Marshall of all
Jerusalem Armies
Old gold
chainmail
Hauberk
& Hood —
Faded blue
Tabard w
Arms of
Jerusalem
Encrusted
Crest
— Simple
belt
— Floating light
djellabah
Old gold chain
legs.

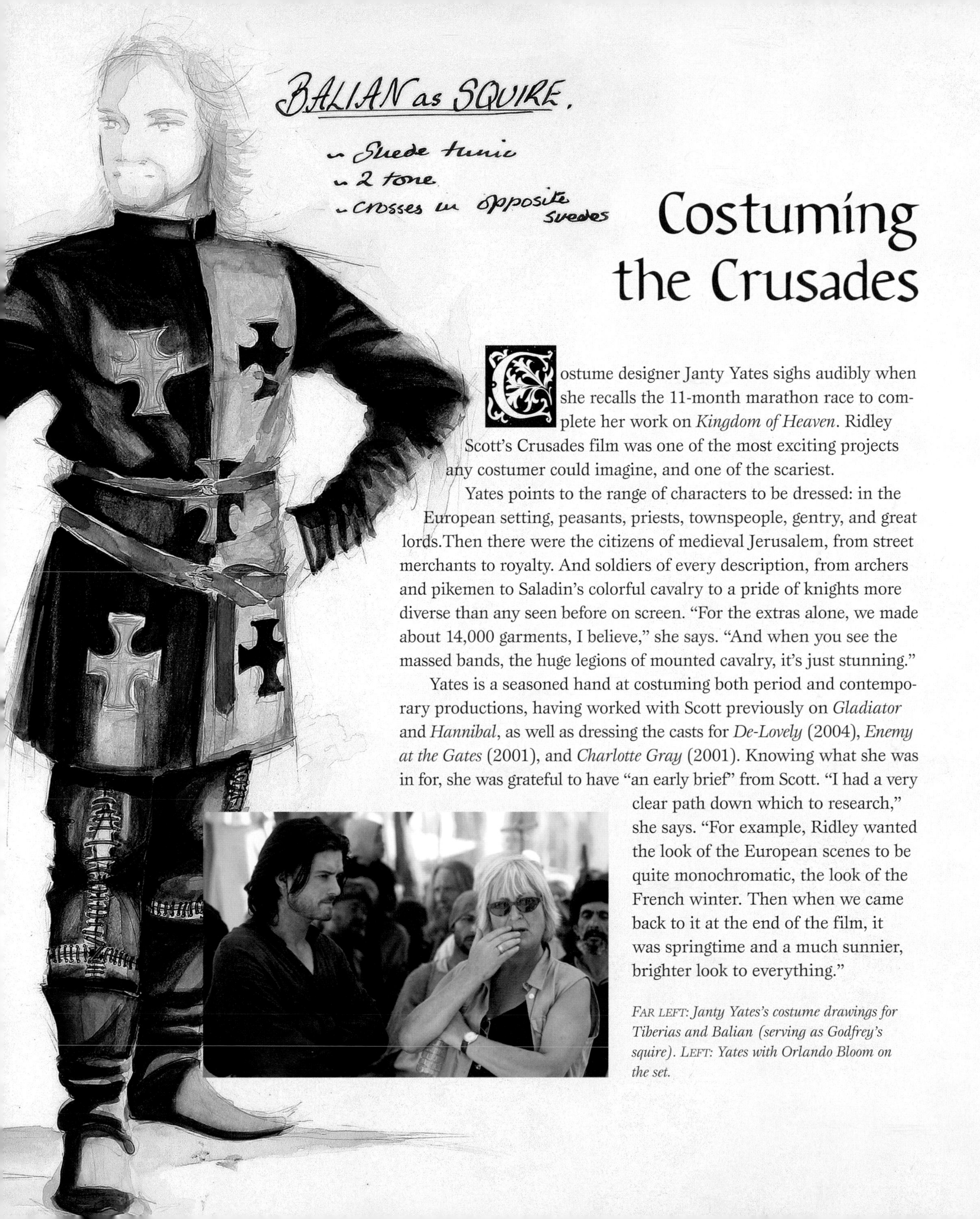

Costuming the Crusades

Costume designer Janty Yates sighs audibly when she recalls the 11-month marathon race to complete her work on *Kingdom of Heaven*. Ridley Scott's Crusades film was one of the most exciting projects any costumer could imagine, and one of the scariest.

Yates points to the range of characters to be dressed: in the European setting, peasants, priests, townspeople, gentry, and great lords.Then there were the citizens of medieval Jerusalem, from street merchants to royalty. And soldiers of every description, from archers and pikemen to Saladin's colorful cavalry to a pride of knights more diverse than any seen before on screen. "For the extras alone, we made about 14,000 garments, I believe," she says. "And when you see the massed bands, the huge legions of mounted cavalry, it's just stunning."

Yates is a seasoned hand at costuming both period and contemporary productions, having worked with Scott previously on *Gladiator* and *Hannibal*, as well as dressing the casts for *De-Lovely* (2004), *Enemy at the Gates* (2001), and *Charlotte Gray* (2001). Knowing what she was in for, she was grateful to have "an early brief" from Scott. "I had a very clear path down which to research," she says. "For example, Ridley wanted the look of the European scenes to be quite monochromatic, the look of the French winter. Then when we came back to it at the end of the film, it was springtime and a much sunnier, brighter look to everything."

FAR LEFT: Janty Yates's costume drawings for Tiberias and Balian (serving as Godfrey's squire). LEFT: Yates with Orlando Bloom on the set.

Coats of Arms

"Research, research, and then more research," laughs Yates, in describing her first stage of work. "I visited every museum that had pertinent collections, every website, also lots of churches and cathedrals, took brass rubbings, and so on. And of course we checked every costume house to see what could be rented rather than made–not much, as it turned out."

The British Museum and the Victoria and Albert provided good examples of the 19th-century painting styles she knew to look for. But the real treasure trove, as for production design, was the Salle de Croisades in Versailles. When Yates was in Paris visiting costume houses, she decided to make her pilgrimage.

"So we troop out there and it could have been such a waste–when we arrived, the room was shut and no curators were around. I begged the supervisor; said we'd come all the way from England. They finally found some poor mug who took us through this creaking door into a baronial hall and four smaller rooms, with what must have been 150 paintings, some as large as 10 by 15 feet. They were painted on walls, painted in recesses of windows."

Yates was amazed to see on those walls the original paintings she had seen in many books they were using for reference. She ran around taking pictures and making copious notes and sketches. But there was a further discovery to be made: "Just as we were leaving I realized that there were hundreds of family crests, maybe thousands–literally framing every painting, on the ceiling, in every nook and cranny." She cadged a little extra time to study these "because we were really stumped for what to do about Balian's family coat of arms."

Designing heraldic motifs for the various knights was one of Yates's major tasks. "Obviously the Templar crest was easy, and the Hospitaler, but for Balian and Godfrey's family, we thought we would just have to invent something. But at the very last window I looked at, there was an extraordinarily beautiful crest–a Maltese cross in burgundy on a gold background–on which was written "Balian 1180." It was just amazing; we started dancing around like mad fiends. It didn't matter that if it was the Balian or not, because it was the right name and exactly the right period." This design was adapted for the Ibelin livery seen in the film.

Chainmail from China

To create a unified look for characters, physical environments, and weaponry, Yates coordinated with the set decoration and armory departments. For example, costume was responsible for the knights' basic armor and helmets, while armory supplied the sword belt and scabbard. Foot soldiers' costumes would be completed by pikes, spears, or bows, also created by armory.

The crossover with set dressing had mainly to do with establishing the heraldic crests. "For costumes, we embroidered the crests onto tabards or surcoats, then we'd attach them in smaller places, such as on the backs of gloves." Set decoration would translate the crests onto banners and shields and other set accoutrements.

FAR LEFT: Imad costumed as a Saracen knight, with an engraved silver helmet, chainmail hauberk, and lavishly embroidered surcoat. INSET PHOTO: Detail of a chainmail hood from a reference painting; seen on page 30. LEFT: Costume for a Saracen warrior. ABOVE: Ghassan Massoud as Saladin and Alexander Siddig as Imad wear different types of mail armor.

Knightly Garb

The late-12th-century knights seen in *Kingdom of Heaven* wear the armor of that period, which was based on the long chainmail hauberk. Only later, in the 14th century, was chainmail replaced or augmented by the full-body plate armor in what we usually picture knights.

Chainmail

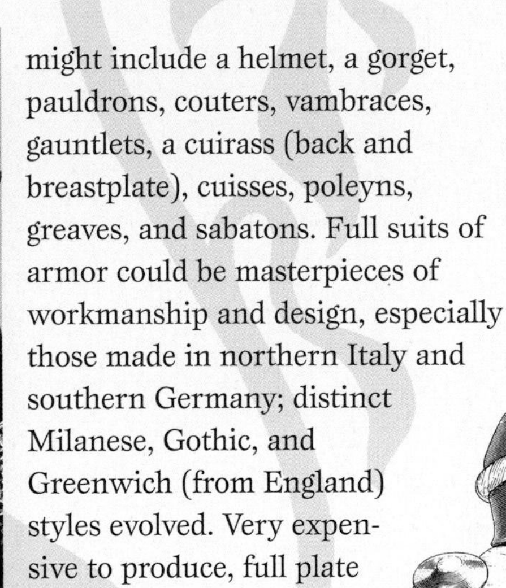

From the English "chain" and the French "*maille*" (net): armor made from small metal rings patterned to form a mesh. Invented some time in the first millennium B.C., possibly in Japan and Europe about the same time; some of the oldest examples are Etruscan. Used prominently throughout the High Middle Ages, when full body suits of mail were developed. Patterns of linking the rings varied between Europe and Asia. Historically the rings would be riveted shut, to reduce the chance of their splitting open when struck hard by sword or arrow. Mail can be punctured by a spear or shorn by a heavy axe or sword blow, but by preventing wounds that broke the skin, it increased the wearer's chance for survival.

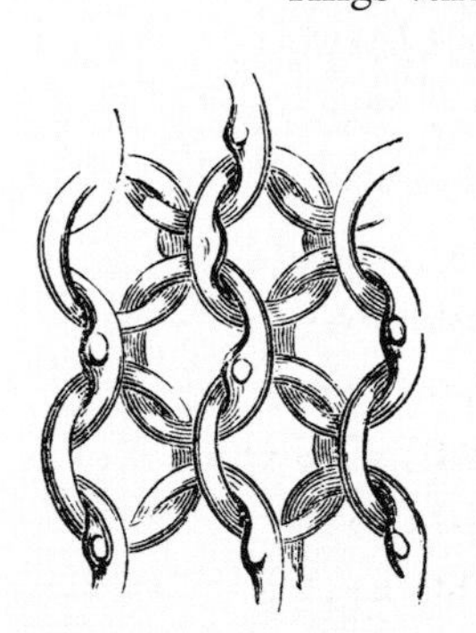

Plate armor

In the 14th century plate began to replace mail, though a mail shirt might still be worn underneath to protect the joints and groin. Pieces might include a helmet, a gorget, pauldrons, couters, vambraces, gauntlets, a cuirass (back and breastplate), cuisses, poleyns, greaves, and sabatons. Full suits of armor could be masterpieces of workmanship and design, especially those made in northern Italy and southern Germany; distinct Milanese, Gothic, and Greenwich (from England) styles evolved. Very expensive to produce, full plate armor was restricted to the rich; lavishly decorated suits stayed in fashion with 17th-century nobles and generals long after ceasing to be militarily useful. Evolution of plate armour triggered developments in the design of offensive weapons and swordfighting technique. While it looks heavy, a full plate armour set could be as light as 45 pounds if well made of tempered steel. The weight was so well spread over the body that a fit man could run, or jump into his saddle.

Surcoat

From French "over the cotta": a long, wide coat sometimes reaching to the feet, with or without sleeves. From about the 12th century, knights wore long and flowing surcoats over their armor. Often emblazoned with the arms of the wearer (whence the term "coat of arms"), they had slits in the bottom front and back for riding. Surcoats helped protect mail from being heated by direct sun and identified the knight by his arms.

Camail

Skirt of mail attached to an armored headpiece that defends the neck from attack.

Hauberk

A mail shirt, generally extending down to defend the legs. The main defense for both body and legs until the late 13th century.

Tabard

Worn over or instead of a surcoat, a cloth tunic or short coat, usually sleeveless, worn by knights over their armor. Could be plain or bear a coat of arms.

Many costumes and most of the fancy hand embroidery of crests and other decoration were done in India, much of it in gold bullion thread. Parisian makers produced most of the surcoats worn by Saracen soldiers: "the most fabulous skirted surcoats cut virtually on a three-quarters circle, in different colors," says Yates. She had boot and shoe and other leather makers working in Morocco and Italy, and independent costume houses in the U.K. filling in what the production's shop couldn't handle.

"We had a very big workshop in England to start out," notes Yates. "My staff there included the chief cutter and six principal makers, a chief 'crowd cutter' and 15 makers doing costumes for secondary leads and crowds. Sometimes there would be up to 10 breaker-downers and distressers (to make costumes look appropriately worn or aged as needed)." Partway through the process, key members of the costume team moved to Spain and Morocco to establish shops on the scene.

Making duplicates of key costumes added to the total effort. "For major characters we might have up to eight repeats of a costume; for others we could get away with three or four," Yates says. "Then you've got your stuntmen, riders, and fighters who might need to be clean and bloody, or bloody and muddy—lots of variations. Once you got blood on a costume you couldn't use that one again."

Creating all the armor was a production in itself. Yates remembers, "We cranked up some of the armor makers who had worked on *Gladiator*, and found other sources wherever we could. A lot of the originals were made in Prague and then duplicated. Once armor started coming in we had 10 to 15 chainmail cutters and alterers working in the shop."

The discovery Yates is proudest of was a new process for making extremely lightweight and realistic-looking chainmail out of plastic. She worked with the fabricators at Weta Workshop Ltd. in New Zealand—the company responsible for all the armor, prosthetic suits, and special makeup effects on the *Lord of the Rings* trilogy—to develop the technique. A brand-new Weta shop based in China made this "miracle mail."

Says Yates, "The plastic chainmail was wonderful for the hot climate in Morocco because it's feather-light. We only used it for principals and stunt performers because it was expensive and we could only get limited amounts," says Yates. "For the crowds we had more economical aluminum chainmail made in India."

Even with such resources, Yates kept her fingers crossed against any major delays or foul-ups in costume production and fitting. "It was very close to the edge."

While shoot was going on, Yates and her team of dressers were constantly on hand to get actors suited up for their day's work. For a fully outfitted knight, this involved 23 separate costume pieces and could take up to 45 minutes.

"Those poor actors," Yates recalls. "First we'd put them in their britches and shirts, then over that went an armored jacket, then the chainmail hauberk. After that they'd put on boots, then we'd lace them into chainmail leggings. Over the hauberk went the embroidered cloth tabard, then the sword belt and scabbard.

"On their head they'd have an armored cap, with the camail. Then a hood, and the helmet fitted over it. Last was usually chainmail gauntlets and a cloak over all." For some of the leads there was even another layer: a beautiful silk surcoat that went under the armored jacket.

"After performing in all this for several hours they were completely numb, but there were hardly any complaints," she marvels. "They were so patient—I think because they knew they looked 'the business.' And if we had taken shortcuts, the effect just wouldn't have been the same."

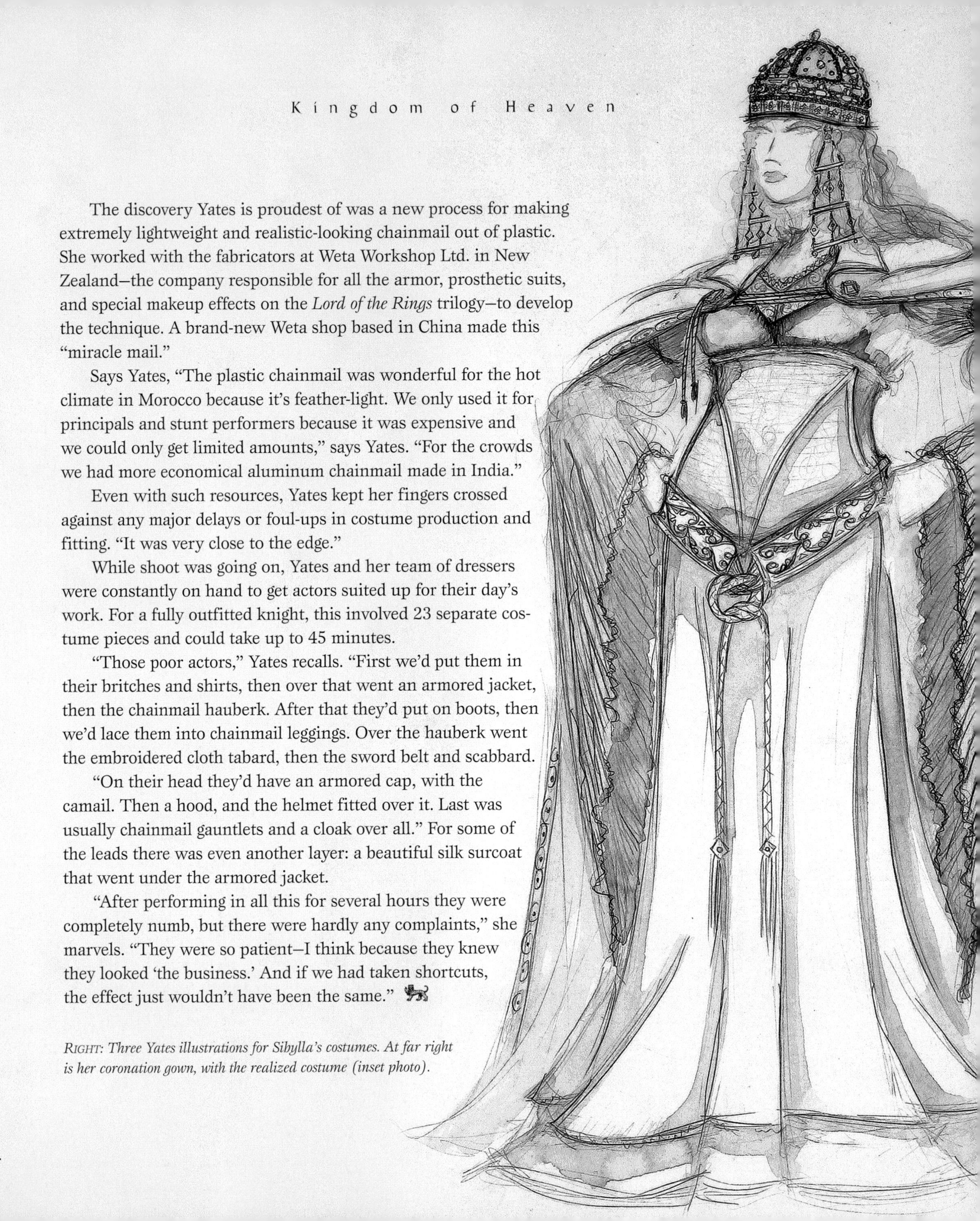

RIGHT: Three Yates illustrations for Sibylla's costumes. At far right is her coronation gown, with the realized costume (inset photo).

SIBYLLA
Riding

Weapons and Warfare

Warfare in the Middle Ages was no less bloody and terrible than it is today, but it was surrounded by great panoply and ingenious gear and tactics that still fascinate people. Part of the draw is the settings where combatants fought: often meeting at the walls of towering castles and fortified cities.

Despite wanting to dramatize the brief peace during King Baldwin's reign in Jerusalem, Ridley Scott and company recognized that this moment was framed by a vast conflict ebbing and flowing over 200 years. Besides, they shared the general fascination with knightly combat and siege tactics, and knew that audiences would expect them. Warfare could be said to define an "epic" and would be integral to *Kingdom of Heaven*'s story.

To depict battle and siege with his trademark synthesis of realism, outsize scale, historical fidelity, and poetic license, Scott turned to trusted technical colleagues from earlier films such as *Gladiator*, including weapons master Simon Atherton, special effects supervisor Neil Corbould, and stunt coordinator Phil Neilson. Working with other production staff, they created every weapon and and staged every fight on location, from a single arrow to a 50-foot siege tower, and from a brief duel to the 10-day assault on Jerusalem. "What you'll have," promises Scott, "are some unbelievable images of massive fields of battle with many people and huge war machines that are completely real."

Blades and Bashers

Simon Atherton, embarking on his fourth film with Scott, began work with "at least two or three months on research. But meanwhile we can start on a lot of things: like manufacturing shields while researching what designs go on them. The same with swords. We start bashing it out, and then decoration comes as I find more information."

Knowing how many weapons to make starts with knowing how many extras will be used in a scene (versus figures added with CGI). And what weapons each fighter will need. "In all we've made equipment for, I should say, at least two and a half thousand people: archers, crossbowmen, shield carriers, spear carriers, and more," says Atherton.

Much of the labor in weapons-making is giving each piece the proper look of long use in action. Many items can be machine-produced, "but then we've had to age it down to make it look made by hand," says Atherton. One staff member spent the better part of three months just painting shields to create a texture. "It takes many layers to create the effects we wanted, including peeling and flaking. As if a knight had his own livery on the shield, but then gone off to crusade and painted over it with a different design. Once we got to Morocco the dust and sand and sun helped a lot with the look of the shields," he adds. "As soon as you arrive, you lay it down on the floor and kick sand and muck all over it—it takes on a good look."

The variety of designs on shields was consciously kept to a minimum to avoid visual confusion. "In reality there would have been a lot of more different liveries, but we stuck to about six: the Ibelin crest, the Templars, the Hospitalers, the Teutonic Knights (another military order), the Knights of Jerusalem (the king's men), and the Saracens."

Swords, that symbol of a knight's vow, were a

War was always the supreme vocation for the knights in the Holy Land, whether they were sincerely pious Crusaders or not. When they met an enemy as superbly skilled in their favourite occupation as the great Saracen leader Saladin, they tended to see him as another knight. Such an attitude was often mutual.... [D]espite being the Crusaders' most deadly enemy, Saladin was said to have been dubbed a knight by his foes, while a nephew of his was knighted (although certainly without any Christian ceremony) by Richard Lionheart himself in response to a request. The crusader knights could not convert a man like Saladin or his nephew to Christianity but they could pronounce them members of the knightly caste.

– Raymond Rudorff,
Knights and the Age of Chivalry

major focus of Atherton's work. Most were cast from very high-grade aluminum, which proved durable and chip-resistant as well as realistic-looking. It's also easier for actors to work with than heavier metals, and somewhat safer. "I try and work in real material rather than plastics, because if it breaks I can repair it–in this case with silver solder rather than just superglue. And it survives, it works."

Sword hilts, made from scratch via a lost-wax casting process, were often personalized for the character and beautifully decorated. (See sidebar on next page.) The blade could be changed out for various purposes: from a standard blade to one made of rubber, or a breakaway blade. Atherton would build according to what the character would be doing with his sword. "We make a mannequin first and go through the moves: run up and down stairs, climb over things with the sword on, see if we can get on and off the horse. Does it stab the side of the horse when you're riding? Does it hit the ground before you do when you get off? We try to solve all the questions the actor might ask us up front."

ABOVE: Allan Smith, one of the film's two sword masters (as well as Orlando Bloom's stunt double), rehearses the swordfight in which Balian and Guy finally have it out. Marton Csokas as Guy (in white tabard) watches. BELOW: Balian with shieldmen and pikemen defending Jerusalem.

Besides swords, other bladed weapons produced by Atherton's

Two Special Swords

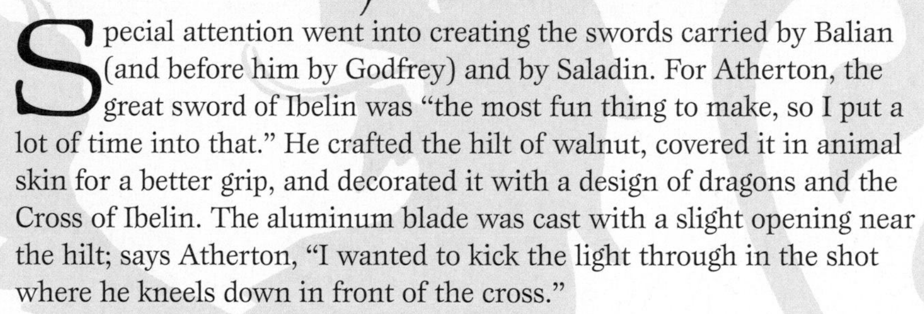

Special attention went into creating the swords carried by Balian (and before him by Godfrey) and by Saladin. For Atherton, the great sword of Ibelin was "the most fun thing to make, so I put a lot of time into that." He crafted the hilt of walnut, covered it in animal skin for a better grip, and decorated it with a design of dragons and the Cross of Ibelin. The aluminum blade was cast with a slight opening near the hilt; says Atherton, "I wanted to kick the light through in the shot where he kneels down in front of the cross."

It took him a week to make the first prototype, between casting silver pieces for the hilt, fitting the pieces, and perfecting the decoration—"Getting the skin to dry in the right way, and the stitching to work." They ended up making five Godfrey swords in all. "There are slightly shorter ones for certain fight sequences, the very shiny 'hero' ones, and the lightweight. And a specific one for riding."

The design of Saladin's sword occasioned a slight tussle with the director, who had in mind a wickedly curved scimitar like those often shown in later paintings of Saracens. Atherton's research, however, showed that Saracen blades were straight during this period. "The Victorians romanticized it," says the weapons master. "So you'll see a few curved swords in the film, but they don't curve that much." Saladin's sword is straight, but it clearly signals that its owner is dangerous: the bone handle is carved with snakes' heads and covered in (imitation) snakeskin, and the business end is forked like a serpent's tongue.

The swords of the historical Balian and Saladin may have contrasted even more. As knights' armor was strengthened over time, the Franks' swords had evolved too. Earlier European swordsmiths had turned out flexible masterpieces of forged and plaited wire—but by the end of the 12th century, Crusader swords were heavy and rigid, meant to pierce armor, but also brittle and easily broken. The most famous swords of the time came from Damascus, where artisans twisted and retwisted metal and hammered it into wafer-thin layers. These swords of "Damascus steel" were self-sharpening as particles came off the edge during use. It was said that Saladin's fine blade could slice through silk floating in the air.

LEFT: Balian uses Godfrey's sword to slay a Saracen lord who attacks him soon after he is shipwrecked in the Holy Land.

shop included falchions (a single-edged European sword of the time, with a curved cutting edge like a machete), as well as daggers and axes. "We had six or seven different kinds of axes, including some rubber ones–which you want when people are laying into each other at close quarters."

Then there was a full array of impact weapons such as maces and flails. (A flail is that nasty-looking stick with a spiked ball attached by a short chain, which could generate more force than a simple mace.) And pole weapons: lances for the mounted knights, spears and pikes for the Saracen cavalry and infantry, respectively.

Bowmen of various kinds played a key role in crusading warfare, and they are well represented in the film. Frankish commanders soon realized that their precious knights were vulnerable to the swift, harassing attacks of Saracen cavalry, who had no compunction about killing the enemy's horses under them. So they formed heavy infantry brigades of trained and armored bowmen, who made effective use of the longbow well before it came into use on the battlefields of Europe.

For their part, the Saracens' most deadly fighters were Turkish cavalry, superb horsemen descended from the raiders of the central Asian steppes, who fought with short bows from their light but sturdy and maneuverable mounts. The essence of Crusades combat was power (the heavy knights) against speed. Both sides also made deadly use of the crossbow.

"Archery's been really good fun on this," says Atherton. "We made lots of bows, including plenty of our good old English longbows. We made about 250 crossbows, with a somewhat unique design and firing mechanism; we simplified it a bit. The Saracen bows were great as well. Every bow works," he adds proudly, "and they're all properly made."

They came on in an irresistible charge on horses swifter than eagles, and urged them on like lightning and, as they advanced, they raised a cloud of dust so that the sky was darkened.... Our people, so few in number, were so hemmed in by the multitudes of the Saracens that they had no means of escape.... Then you might have seen our troopers, having lost their chargers, marching on foot with the archers or casting missiles from their arbalests [a kind of crossbow] or arrows from bows against the enemy and repelling their attacks in the best way they were able. The Turks, skilled in the bow, pressed ceaselessly upon them.

— Anonymous chronicler of the Third Crusade

ABOVE: Final composed frame of Saladin preparing his army for the battle of Hattin.

Arrows were made in mass quantities, close to 20,000 in Atherton's estimate. Besides those used by individual bowmen, many were shot from catapults during the siege scenes, creating a virtual rain of arrow onto the city. A striking effect was created with flaming arrows as well. Atherton explains:

"You've got to use a real arrow, and it has to have a real flame on it, so we make a wad up. You can't fire real flaming arrows too far around the set, though, so it's very controlled. You see the real arrows being nocked and fired, leaving the bow, and then the CGI ones take over to get the range needed." Flaming arrows were expensive to make and the firemen couldn't always get to them in time to put them out. "So we started covering them in tinfoil, to stop them burning up."

Scott would often drop by and admire the latest creations. "He likes what we make and usually has a specific look that he wants and will push for. I tend to show him a lot of things in progress. He'll pop along and say what he likes, or you can drop in and give him a preview. He's always got time to look at things." Scott confirms simply, "I love seeing the arrows and all the gear being built."

The Art of the Siege

More than any other kind of hostile encounter, the siege typified warfare during the Crusades. Control of territory and travel routes in the Holy Land was critical. To hold Jerusalem the Crusaders needed unimperiled access to the Mediterranean, and whoever possessed the walled cities on the coast and the fortresses inland controlled the surrounding lands and passages.

As the knights of the First Crusade descended on Jerusalem, they successfully besieged and conquered important fortified towns such as Nicaea and Antioch. They used all the techniques learned by European experience: blockade, starving the enemy into surrender; siege machines and escalade; undermining or setting fire to city walls—and when none of those worked, sometimes ruse or bribery. From the Byzantines they adopted Greek fire: pots of a highly flammable mixture of sulfur, resin, and other substances that could be hurled with deadly effect.

To soften up the defenses, attackers would pound the daunting walls and the people inside with missiles from a variety of powerful catapults, sometimes for days (see sidebar on next page). And when it came time for a manned assault, they would push a movable siege tower, or several of them, up against the enemy's walls at vulnerable points, enabling attackers to reach the top of the walls with some protection.

These great throwing machines and "siege engines," as the towers were called, featured prominently in the original conquest of Jerusalem by the First Crusade, and in Saladin's recapture of it in 1187. Because they were so heavy to move, they were nearly always built on site; the First Crusaders came close to failing because Jerusalem's commander had cleared all the timber anywhere near the city. But a fleet arrived from Genoa in the nick of time with timbers and supplies, and several siege engines were built.

Not as much detail exists on the specific tactics used in Saladin's later siege of Jerusalem, but it's known that his army built siege engines that were destroyed by Balian's defenders. In the end it was

RIGHT: Guillaume de Clermont defending Ptolemais (Acre) in 1291, *by Dominique Louis Papety, 1845—another of the paintings used as reference.*

Saladin's overwhelming manpower that forced the city's capitulation.

These impressive, visually dramatic machines would feature prominently in the film's siege. Charged with manufacturing them was the practical special effects team led by Neil Corbould, another Scott veteran of *Gladiator* and *Black Hawk Down*. "The Crusades have always interested me because of the big siege weapons," Corbould affirms. "We made three big siege towers, two trebuchets, and a couple of mangonels. We have 12 ladders that come in at a certain point. But of course that's just the minimum we needed to get on film. Once the CGI team does its work, it will look like many more."

The historical towers were built about as high the walls they were attacking (sometimes higher to allow archers to fire downward into the city). Their rectangular wooden superstructure was covered with animal skins soaked in vinegar to resist fire, and they rolled on huge wheels, pushed and pulled into position by many men. The towers made for *Kingdom* were 50 to 60 feet high and detailed with great historical fidelity. A system of cables, pulleys, and hydraulic winches helped move them into position, though extras actually pushed them as well.

The tower's base often housed an iron-headed battering ram with its crew of operators. On platforms midway up crouched archers and crossbowmen. And from the top level a footbridge could be lowered onto the wall so that foot soldiers, clambering up an interior stair, could pour into the besieged city. The towers' size and threat potential made them obvious targets for projectiles and Greek fire launched by the defenders.

Corbould decided to build the towers and other siege machines with authentic designs and material "so that when men are pushing these 25-ton structures, they're going to be pushing them for real." He went to Canada to fabricate the pieces of his siege engines—the heftiest timbers were 1 by 2 feet thick. They were assembled on site, much like their the originals. "In making these machines, we've gone back in technology in some respects," he notes. "To make a modern hydraulic ram that would perform like the old siege machines would probably cost a hundred thousand dollars. Instead we just built them for real. There's no point in trying to alter the design when something works already."

Beware Flying Objects

Scott acknowledges a distinct fondness for medieval machines that hurl rocks and other objects hundreds of feet through the air. "Our trebuchet that we built has an arm that pivots some 56 feet. It could take 100 pounds of rock and sling it 400 meters. The first time one of my effects guys says, 'Okay, knock the pin out,' we all stood there gobsmacked as it threw a big stone ball about 150 yards. It was pretty impressive."

But such machines were serious business in medieval warfare, used to batter walls or throw projectiles over them, or sometimes to launch steel grappling hooks. The general category of "catapults" actually included several kinds of projectile-throwing machines, which differ according to how they store and release propulsion energy. A simple *tensional catapult* (developed from the Roman *ballista*) uses a member under tension to propel the throwing arm, much like a giant crossbow. Later torsional catapults included the *mangonel*, which has an arm with a bucket or cup at one end to hold the projectile. The bottom end of the throwing arm is attached to rope or fibers that are twisted, providing the force when released. Simon Atherton observed of the film's mangonels: "You can get a lot of range, but it takes six or seven men to fire them. You'll see them in the courtyard at Jerusalem, lobbing large boulders and flaming pots toward the Saracens."

The most sophisticated catapult was a *trebuchet* (from the French *trebuchier*, "to overthrow"),

which used gravity to propel the throwing arm. A falling counterweight pulls down the bottom end of the arm, and the projectile is thrown from a bucket, sometimes attached to a rope at the top end of the arm. It's been compared to a sling attached to a giant see-saw.

Trebuchets could reduce cities to rubble, as they were able to strike from far away where arrows could not reach their operators. Objects thrown might include large stones, cows, or even rejected negotiators. Rotting flesh (to introduce disease) and barrels of burning tar or oil (to burn the defenders) were also popular. The largest trebuchets had a range of up to a quarter-mile—very similar to the ones built for *Kingdom*.

Far left: Arthur Max's sketch of the Jerusalem siege. Left: Illustration of a trebuchet from the Encyclopédie Médiévale, *used in the film's re-creation. Right: The working trebuchet. Below: Final frame with siege towers and trebuchets.*

Staging the Fights

Kingdom of Heaven enacts a lively range of the kinds of fighting that went on in the medieval Near East, from hand-to-hand combat to the multi-day siege.

The mounted charge of heavy knights was always the Crusaders' preferred tactic, usually successful as long as the enemy remained massed in place to take its impact. Such charges have reliably supplied thrills in countless period films, and Scott wasn't about to miss his chance. Since the battle of Hattin wasn't filmed, he used the opportunity of Saladin's attack on the fortress of Kerak.

Hand-to-hand combat in close quarters could be brutal or artful—sometimes both, as shown in closeups of the siege fighting and in a scene where Balian is ambushed by Guy's assassins. This and Balian's final confrontation with Guy make good showcases for swordplay.

The climactic siege of Jerusalem depicts the usual elements of siege warfare as practiced in the Holy Land: the deadly bombardment of the city by Saladin's machines outside the walls; the defenders returning fire from their own machines and from archers on the walls; Greek fire being dumped from giant pots onto the attackers; and the final assault by the siege towers.

Ridley Scott describes details of the action as the towers advance: "You see the machine being pushed up to the walls, how it was surrounded by archers and shieldmen protecting the pushers and the soldiers being transported in the tower. The archers and shieldmen alternate places so that archers could nock a new arrow in safety."

Gasp-inducing shots show men on the towers being hit with flaming oil and falling. Notes Scott, "The stuntmen wore protective clothing, of course, and were covered in gel. For the shot, they would be drenched in kerosene, then hit with flaming arrows, and fall 45 feet onto cardboard boxes—being careful not to fall on top of each other, which could be fatal."

The film's pyrotechnic effects were legion. Says Corbould, "We've got siege weapons firing, or sometimes blowing up. We had to do a lot of explosions in Jerusalem: fireball hits, rock hits." The number of cameras needed to cover the action added to his challenge. "They're shooting between five and eight cameras on each take, and we needed to get an effect in each one of them."

The work is painstaking and time-consuming, if only because of safety issues. Scores of stuntmen and upwards of 800 extras must be in exactly the right places when the explosions are going off. "We rehearse until we get it right," says Corbould. "It takes us a good two or three hours to rig up one shot like this, accounting for all the cameras."

"The biggest risk is obviously fire effects," he notes, "because we we were using liquid propane as well as petrol and diesel fuels. The risk of burns is very serious, so every precaution is taken to make sure it's a safe environment for the crew."

For the siege scene, Corbould's team laid a four-inch-wide "ring burn" all around the set. "We've put in close to a kilometer of gas pipe, and we'll probably go through about a 120,000 liters by the end of the shoot." Different fuels are used depending on the desired effect. "If they want it smoky with less fire we use diesel. If they want a cleaner flame, we mix alcohol with petrol."

Story demands put the film's star, Orlando Bloom, right in the line of fire. Again, rehearsal and precise timing were the keys to safety. "First we run it through with stunts," explains Corbould, "and

> The Frankish charge was renowned and feared throughout the Middle East.... The attack of the medieval horsemen, though it relied for its effect on the collective mass of its participants, was essentially an aggregate of many individual charges; it depended for its success on impact with an enemy who, in resisting, would be shattered by its weight. If the enemy, like the Turks, was able to remove itself from its path, then the Franks, their formation loosening as they advanced, were vulnerable to counter-attack. Nor, after their original charge, could they be any longer controlled by their commander.... The elusive tactics of the Turks set the Franks the problem of timing the charge, which was their most powerful tactical weapon, so that it succeeded in making contact with the main body of the enemy.
>
> – R. C. Smail, Crusading Warfare

then once we get Orlando on the set, we run him through it step-by-step. We may do two or three rehearsals to make sure that he's in the right place and comfortable. Sometimes we'd show him video tests which gives us all a sense of what's going to happen, and it helps us for safety. There's a very fine line between getting a great effect or a complete disaster."

In all this work SFX collaborates closely with stunt coordinator Phil Nielson. Says Corbould, "We've been on several of Ridley's movies together and have a strong working relationship. Phil's always involved with how we set things up, and his knowledge of what we do helps him place people where they are safe."

Nothing in *Kingdom* is done merely for effect, he notes. "Ridley has a unique way of incorporating our work into his films so that it feels completely organic and not just like showing off. He makes it part of the story; we're just complementing his storytelling."

The Vision Lives

Principal photography for *Kingdom of Heaven* wrapped in Morocco in June 2004, but a long road lay ahead: nearly a year of postproduction work before the official release date of May 6, 2005. The road would contain many twists and turns: getting the final cut to a manageable length, decisions on story elements to retain or not, and a change of composers, among them.

From this point on, Ridley Scott's chief creative collaborator would be film editor Dody Dorn. If the work of the production designer kick-starts the physical production, and the DP is the key creative during the shoot, the editor is third in this triumvirate of experts a director most relies on. Typically the last to come on board—sometimes only a week or so before the shoot begins—the editor is also among the last on hand as the production winds down. "I think all the people working in these roles with Ridley," says Dorn, "would say that the relationship is really about manifesting the director's vision."

Along with cutting the film—which involves relatively few individuals—the major postproduction effort for a film like *Kingdom* is creating and incorporating all the visual effects shots it requires. That process would call on the talents of hundreds, under the leadership of visual effects supervisor Wesley Sewell and visual effects producer Victoria Alonso. During post, editing and VFX were intimately linked in every way, sharing office space and computer networks so they could track each others' work hour by hour and frame by frame.

It's misleading to imagine production and post-production as isolated phases, though. In fact, the task of planning and executing VFX began well before the shoot, and Dorn was on hand during nearly the whole of principal photography, viewing dailies and editing film—so that a substantial part of her work was completed even before the wrap date.

Visual Magic

Attaining epic scale in today's cinema invariably means making use of the incredibly sophisticated computer technology available to bring forth sets and action of breathtaking scope, complexity, and realism. And indeed there were aspects of *Kingdom* that Scott meant to be breathtakingly big and complex: medieval Jerusalem, the opposing forces arrayed before Kerak, and of course the final siege.

But as spectacular as some of the effects are, their creators say they are not an end but rather a means to serve the story and the director's vision of another time and place. "We have one of the best directors and cinematographers working today, and we're working into their world, in terms of light and color and composition– trying to make the photography they create absolutely look beautiful," says Wes Sewell. "Our larger goal is to use the latest and best technology to reach a new level of realism, photographically and interactively."

Or as Dody Dorn puts it: "This is first big VFX film I've edited, but this is a reality-based narrative, not a fantasy. This film has a naturalistic style that flows into the VFX arena–the effects are meant to be invisible, and are. I've really appreciated Ridley's aesthetic in the way he uses effects as part of his whole composition–rather than doing something just because he can."

Still, "big" is an operative word for the VFX in *Kingdom*: more than 1,000 shots were created digitally. Sewell–who served as visual effects editor on several earlier Scott films–had a crew of eight technicians working on location as he designed and plotted out concepts with Scott, cinematographer John Mathieson, and the physical effects group led by Neil Corbould. Eventually several hundred VFX artists would be working at the several effects facilities engaged by him and Alonso to execute various shots–chief among these being London's Moving Picture Company, located near the team's Soho offices.

The VFX shots sorted into categories according to the film's needs. One category might be described as multiplication: where several hundred extras portraying foot soldiers or cavalry are transformed into many thousands of highly realistic bodies. Inanimate objects proliferated as well: whereas three siege towers and two trebuchets were built "practically," up to 100 siege machines may be seen on the screen–not all at once, but in different numbers depending on the shot width and angle. "The numbers weren't arbitrary," notes Sewell. "Ridley is always composing for the frame, for that moment in time. When we add something, we add it according to what he visualizes."

In an earlier age of filmmaking, Sewell observes, "you might have had anywhere from 3,000 to 10,000 extras on hand to create big crowd scenes or battles. But that's not going to really satisfy when you're meant to have somewhere around three hundred thousand.

"Today we have the technology to create vast multitudes of people that look very real and move and interact with each other realistically. We still need a fairly large number of actual bodies, as many as possible. In a wide shot we might get away with using just 10 or 20, and then just populating the shot with computer-generated people. But when you want to get in fairly close, you want to see real people, while in the backgrounds we can

OPPOSITE: Before and after VFX. TOP: Balian and Imad approach Jerusalem. MIDDLE: Refugees flee into Kerak. BOTTOM: Balian on the hill of Golgotha, above Jerusalem.

still use CG people and it won't be apparent. In the case of our big cavalry charge we had more than 600 extras to work with, so that was a luxury."

Sheer numbers are at least as deceptive on the screen as in real life, when the media estimates crowd totals at mass gatherings. More than 1 million CG bodies were added to one shot in order for it to seem as if 200,000 Saracens are attacking Jerusalem. "In shots that are so vast and wide, you lose a sense of quantity and volume," notes Sewell.

The technology at work here does much more than simply cloning bodies, however. "At times we move some of the real people to add CG people, because we want the action to happen in a different way," says Sewell. "It can allow us to 'kill' thousands on a scale that couldn't be done practically, and to introduce great variation in how these CG bodies react and interact."

All this is done with a remarkable new generation of computer-generated simulations—a state-of-the-art technology first developed by Weta Workshop for *Lord of the Rings*. "But the Moving Picture Company has taken this a few steps beyond with their own open-architecture software," says Sewell. "Their simulations have a lot more refinement in how the bodies can move and interact, so we can create a more plausible scenario."

Each "Sim" contains a form of 3-D artificial intelligence, so that each of the hundreds of thousands of CG figures has a kind of 'brain,'" Sewell explains. "They know how to run and not run into someone, or if they do, how to react: sometimes they trip, or fall, or push the other guy away. You set up these 'agents' with certain stimuli or conditions, then just let the computer run and see what happens. You can take out what doesn't work, or refine it—make the game work the way you want."

Features introduced specifically for *Kingdom* allow cloned figures to represent a multiethnic range of people. "The Saracen army has come to Jerusalem from many parts of the Arab world, so we needed to suggest different types," says Sewell. They also can incorporate variation in the figures' uniforms. "In several sessions with costume we photographed every possible arrangement of clothing in a controlled environment to create a library of textures that can be applied to the computer models. Once we had our standards set, we could easily change the color of a turban or a tunic. So you'll have the impression that some soldiers came from Syria or Egypt or Cyprus, and so on, to join Saladin's army."

Another essential area of VFX was digital sets. "We did, of course, have a massive built set for Jerusalem, which was necessary to shoot a lot of

LEFT: VFX supervisor Wes Sewell and VFX producer Victoria Alonso discuss a shot set-up with Ridley Scott on the Morocco set.

Painting in the Computer

Matte painting is a traditional tool for creating or extending a cinematic picture into the distance. "In the old days," says Sewell, "any sense of depth or 3-D was just an illusion created by a talented artist on a flat painting.

"We have some amazing artists working on this film—the same talent, but these days they work in the computer doing 'two and a half D matte painting.' We make our 3-D model to set up the shadings and lighting and basic shapes, then the artist will literally paint on that model with his electronic tools.

"To paint every side of every structure in this huge virtual city to a realistic level isn't feasible," he continues. "So the artists paint just the surfaces facing the camera. And because it's set up with all our production data in the computer, if the camera does move, the painted model will move with it. Just as if you were walking down a corridor or past a minaret, watching the light change on those surfaces. You get perspective changes and light changes and shadow changes. All these things give life to this artificial re-created city."

the practical action and achieve the texture and atmosphere Ridley wanted," says Sewell. For some shots, VFX were used simply to extend the walls of the practical set and make them curve around in a natural way. But the built set also served as a basis for creating a much larger three-dimensional set in the computer—a virtual city the size of historical Jerusalem at that time.

The city as Scott envisioned it was "a movie version of medieval Jerusalem," as Sewell points out. "The battle that takes place, with armies advancing across a plain to the base of the walls... it doesn't really exist like that. It was Ridley's vision of how he wanted the scene to look. And could only really exist in the computer."

There are basically two options today for creating a fully realized CG set, explains Sewell. "You can build a physical model and photograph it in the right light conditions and right placement, and incorporate that into all the shots where it belongs. But after assessing our needs with Ridley, we decided a better plan was to build our 3-D model in the computer, then use a form of traditional matte painting to detail it." (See sidebar.)

ABOVE: Saladin and Baldwin meet outside Kerak; fortress in background was a 3-D matte painting added in CGI.

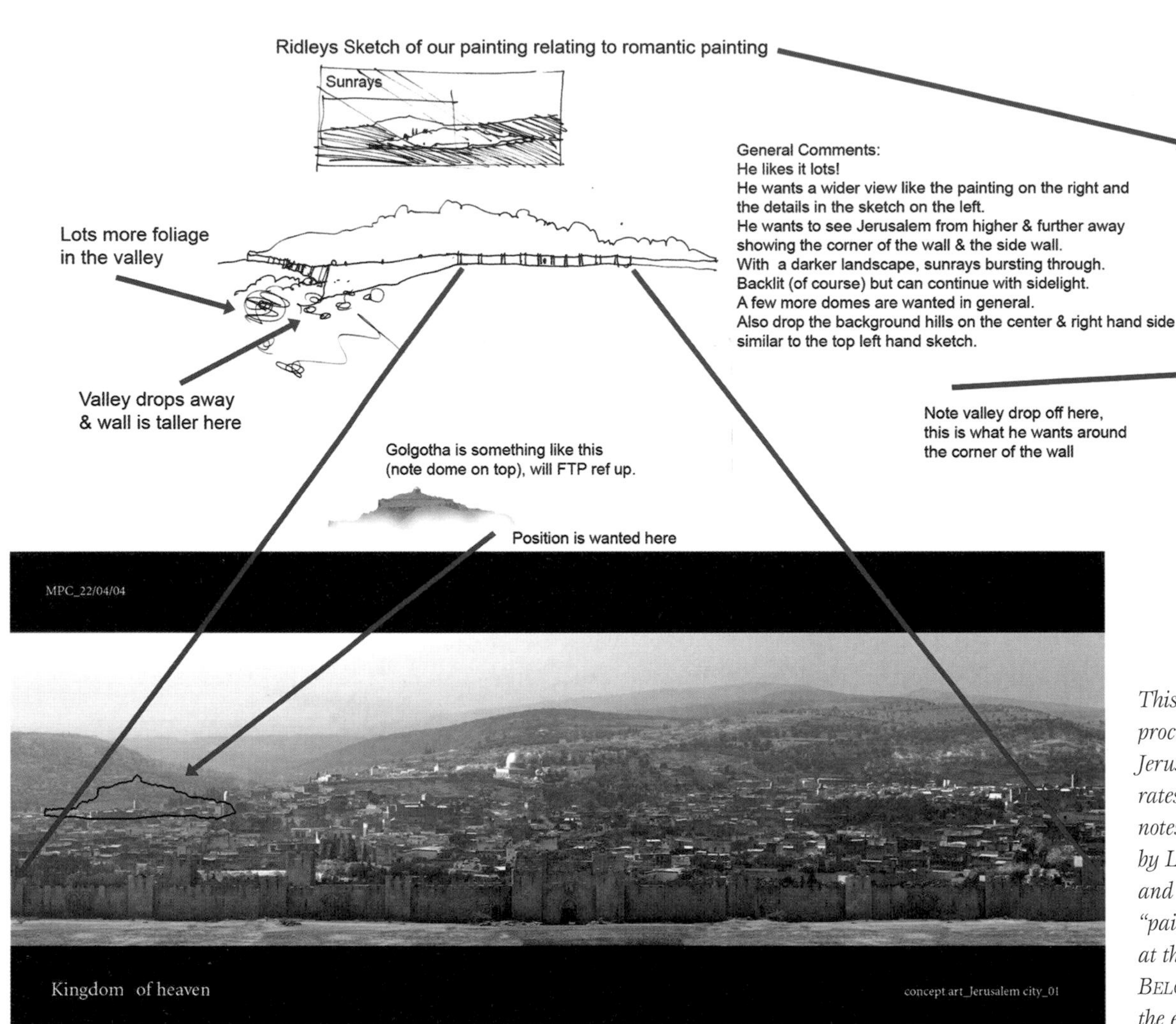

This assemblage traces the process for designing the look of Jerusalem in VFX. It incorporates Ridley Scott's sketches and notes, the 19th-century painting by Löffler used for inspiration, and the VFX team's computer "painting" of the extended set at this point in its evolution. Below: Final frame showing the exodus from Jerusalem.

Along with the virtual set, there exists within the computer(s) a camera that duplicates the moves of the cameras used during production. "While shooting film in production, we have a technician recording the camera's information: how far it is off the ground, how far away from that wall or that market stall or that person. All this data is logged into computer, so when it comes time do a visual effect—to put something into the digital set—it can be correlated with that data. We know what was the focal length on the camera for that event, what the film stock was, etc. So inside the computer are lights, camera, action! The camera in the computer is moving, tracking, dancing around just like it was in production, using these digital coordinates."

A rather magical mirrored ball is key to recording data for the cameras. Held up at various places on the set during production, the ball shows the camera how light is striking every single plane in the vicinity. "It's all about light," says Sewell. "The only way an object created in the computer can look real is to have light bouncing and reflecting off it at the same angle at which we photographed it in reality. And light of the same color and quality.

"What we're recoding is light striking the object from more angles than you can possibly see, wrapping all around it. Later the computer 'unwraps' each frame so the light can be replicated in our 3-D environment, and the CG object or person will look like it lives in this world.

"We can apply those values to any three-dimensional object and make it sit into the scene," he adds. "That's how we can have massive 3-D armies of Saracens or Jerusalemites that are not real, but they can be standing toe to toe with real people and you won't know the difference."

In addition to Jerusalem, the fortress of Kerak was also created as a digital set, through the same process of 3-D modeling and matte painting. Built practically as the reverse face of the Jerusalem set, Kerak was transported in the computer to sit on top of a hill above the battlefield where Balian confronts Saladin's huge force.

During the shoot the VFX team collaborated with practical effects to lay the groundwork for the impressive explosions and bombardments seen during the siege, and the crash of one of the giant siege towers. "Practical effects might begin a shot, like a machine firing, and then VFX will show the object or arrows flying through the air," says Victoria Alonso. "Or, since every explosion must have a cause, VFX will initiate the event by flying a payload through the air digitally—it could be a boulder or a firepot—and then it becomes a physical explosion when it strikes its target."

During the massive bombardment of Jerusalem, hundreds of such payloads filled the sky, an effect that would have been much too dangerous to render in any way but through VFX.

VFX was also used to augment in various ways the action involving real actors. In the foreground of the Kerak cavalry charge, for instance, the charging riders are real but the clash where they meet is composited with VFX plates from different passes, the layers of horses merging together. In the long shots CG riders are added.

In smaller-scale, man-to-man fighting, VFX was used to add subtle or invisible touches. Blood might be added in one place or painted out in another for the sake of composition. An actor's face might be enhanced, or if his sword has a jeweled hilt, a glint of light might strike there at a key instant. "We're always continuing to refine and enhance in every way possible," says Alonso.

That includes God's great outdoors: whole sequences would be relit in CG, or weather phenomena tweaked. Ridley Scott is known to favor dramatic, moody skies, and "there were lots of sky replacements," confirms Alonso. "Some were real skies that we found and photographed at other locations, and put in."

Wes Sewell thinks audiences will be both impressed by and blissfully unaware of the VFX work in *Kingdom*, due to the level of craft

employed and the advances in technology utilized. He credits science for the latter: many of the simulation and rendering tools now available were adapted from applications used for architectural and photorealistic rendering, or that mimic physical properties like gravity and three-dimensionality. "That's where the power and capability came from. And we're using it to make unreal things happen realistically."

The Editing Room

Editor Dody Dorn's first clue that she might be editing *Kingdom of Heaven* was a Christmas gift from Ridley Scott: a hefty art book on Orientalist painters. "I guess it was his way of suggesting that I might be interested in this movie."

Dorn's first project with Scott was *Matchstick Men* (2003), but she is an industry veteran. Her work on Christopher Nolan's *Memento*, with its intricate inverse narrative, won attention not just for her but for the power of editing generally.

She and Scott had already established their communication style, so she could join the production on location without missing a beat. Once shooting began, they had to wait a few days for the first dailies to come in, "but after that we watched dailies every day." Perhaps surprisingly, she stayed away from the set unless Scott wanted her to see something specific. "As fascinating as it is, I prefer to keep some distance from the process and the daily grind: the long hard hours, cold, mud, sand in your face, all the stressful issues that come up. I feel an editor needs objectivity—so when I first see the image on film, it's similar to how an audience member would see it."

Dorn spent most of her days editing. And at the end of Scott's long day of shooting, they would meet to go over dailies—usually with Mathieson and sometimes a producer and Wes Sewell present as well. Viewing footage with Scott was exciting, says Dorn, "because he goes into stream of consciousness talking while watching dailies. He'll talk about what he had in mind for the shot, things he liked in a take—that feather crossing over there or a certain line reading. I try to let the film flow over me but I'm always taking notes."

More than 1.2 million feet of film was shot for

Kingdom, more than twice the amount Dorn had ever worked with. Usually she tries to view dailies alone once, but there was just too much film to watch everything twice.

Viewing the dailies seemed to feed Scott's energy, says Dorn. "He relishes the images and vamps about editorial ideas and effects: 'Let's try this at 8 frames a second'... Slow that down, speed that up... Let's add birds here, we want to add smoke there.' We run the film on a traditional projection system from Arri called Lockpro, so we can make any of these fine viewing adjustments Ridley wants."

When she wasn't viewing or editing film, Dorn was making lists–an important responsibility for the editor. "The lists are things we don't have," she says simply. "It may be a line of dialog that's muffled or a screen direction that's unclear or any one of countless details needed to tell a story in images. On such a huge project it's easy for little things to get lost in the shuffle, and it might turn out to be a vital link in storytelling.

"For example, if the script says that Balian grabs the cross from around the priest's neck and throws him into the fire... well, I may see him reach for the cross, but if I can't tell that it's a cross, the audience wonders, what's he doing throwing the guy in the fire?"

Normally after the production wraps, an editor has a week or two on her own to produce a first cut. But Scott took only a few days off after the wrap, then plunged right back into the editing. "Ridley wanted to get started before I had even finished the initial assembly." When he did need to absent himself later, Dorn finished her first pass.

"You have to start somewhere, and an editor needs to have a kind of fearlessness about going forward. Cutting film is more like sculpting in clay than marble. You can't gather up the marble slivers and start over, but with clay you just keep a damp cloth over the thing and come back to work on it whenever you want."

During post Dorn and Scott usually worked side by side. Scott brought into the editing room his typical openness about collaboration. Unlike other directors, says Dorn, who prefer to operate behind closed doors with an editor, Scott is willing to hear good input from anyone. "He's so self-assured that there's no insecurity or possessiveness about whose idea something is."

ABOVE: Editor Dody Dorn. OPPOSITE and RIGHT: VFX frames of 3-D matte painting of Jerusalem.

Editing around the large number of VFX shots was a challenge. "Because it takes so long to manifest the VFX shots, it disrupts the generally accepted rhythm of cutting film for long-form narrative," Dorn notes. "You can't always do things in the order they come up in the story—some events have to be edited sooner because they need time to create VFX." When the VFX frames come back, Dorn cuts them in and makes adjustments as needed.

Another Scott trait Dorn admires is his readiness to shift gears at any point if a better idea comes along. "He never stops thinking: it's both the pleasure and the bane of working with him. Everything is open to reinterpretation until time runs out. So the challenge is making sure that where you finally land is not quixotic but best fits the design of the film."

As footage was carved away, Dorn worked to highlight the most powerful images. "Ridley drives you into this world with the images," she says. "Many of them are like moving paintings, so rich and lush; you could say expressionistic. They are alive." Even the ones that are hard to take because of blood or violence. "Part of the point is that it's visceral and real, but we're also trying to strike a balance. You want people to see your film, and if the material is alienating, it's counterproductive."

In trying to identify a visual signature for *Kingdom of Heaven*, Dorn feels that it manifests a more naturalistic style than other Scott films. "It's gritty: you can practically smell the caked-on dirt and rabbit grease on the chainmail," she says. "There is a sort of chaos in the fight scenes that feels realistic and unstaged. The light is natural more often than not—especially in exterior wide shots—largely due to multiple camera set-ups.

"He is always trying new things and each film has a visual character all its own."

Worlds of Sound

Typically sound and scoring are done in the final stages of post—although when cutting and VFX work go on for as long as they did in this production, it's impossible to wait until the film is "locked."

"We're scoring now," said Dorn in late January 2005. "Everyone has to work in synch from this point on to get it done in time." This added another major layer of collaboration: with scoring, sound effects editing, ADR recording (automated dialog replacement, formerly known as dialog looping), and mixing.

The musician who has to stay on top of all this is Harry Gregson-Williams, who some call the hottest composer currently working in Hollywood. Hans Zimmer was originally slated to score *Kingdom*, as he has done for most of Scott's films, but scheduling problems arose. Gregson-Williams was fortunately available and his frequent past collaboration with Zimmer was an advantage.

Gregson-Williams has compiled an astonishing resume in his decade or so or film work. Asked what he tries to bring to his assignments, he says, "I'm always looking for a way through to the emotion of the film."

He also brings a unique piece of relevant life experience to *Kingdom*'s Middle East setting. He spent a number of years in North Africa teaching music to children—a phase he considers formative. He learned Arabic and soaked up the distinctive musical idiom of the region, which he's had a chance to draw on for the film's score.

OPPOSITE: Before and after VFX. TOP: Balian and Sibylla outside Kerak. MIDDLE: Balian and a palace guard on the palace terrace overlooking Jerusalem. BOTTOM: 3-D horses and riders replicated for the cavalry charge at Kerak.

Twentieth Century Fox
Presents

A Scott Free Production
A Ridley Scott Film

KINGDOM OF HEAVEN™

ORLANDO BLOOM as Balian

EVA GREEN as Sibylla

JEREMY IRONS as Tiberias

DAVID THEWLIS as The Hospitaler

BRENDAN GLEESON as Reynald

MARTON CSOKAS as Guy de Lusignan

and

LIAM NEESON as Godfrey of Ibelin

Music by HARRY GREGSON-WILLIAMS

Costume Designer JANTY YATES

Film Editor DODY DORN, A.C.E.

Production Designer ARTHUR MAX

Director of Photography
JOHN MATHIESON, B.S.C.

Executive Producers

BRANKO LUSTIG

LISA ELLZEY

TERRY NEEDHAM

Produced by RIDLEY SCOTT

Written by WILLIAM MONAHAN

Directed by RIDLEY SCOTT

www.kingdomofheavenmovie.com

Further Reading and Viewing

Arab Historians of the Crusades
by Francesco Gabrieli. University of California Press; 1984. Paperback, ISBN: 0520052242.
Excerpts from contemporary Arab chronicles of the Crusades include portraits of Saladin and accounts of events spanning several Crusades. The writing, especially that of Saladin's secretary Imad ad-Din, can be florid and hyperbolic but generally offers fascinating new perspectives.

The Atlas of the Crusades
by Jonathan Riley-Smith. Facts on File, 1990. Hardcover, ISBN: 0816021864.
Cambridge professor Riley-Smith is among the chief experts on the Crusades, taking the position that they were ideologically justified—or at least inevitable—to medieval European Christians. This unique oversize volume features superb maps and other visual tools for understanding the geopolitics of the era as well as military events and everyday life.

Chronicles of the Crusades: Eye-Witness Accounts of the Wars Between Christianity and Islam
by Elizabeth Hallam. Welcome Rain Publishers, 2000. Paperback, ISBN: 1566491932.
The author, a fellow of the Royal Historical Society, weaves together selections from medieval chroniclers representing Western, Byzantine, and Muslim views on the Crusades with expert commentary and short biographies of key figures. Readable translations help bring the primary documents to life.

A Concise History of the Crusades
by Thomas F. Madden. Rowman & Littlefield Publishers, 1999. Paperback, ISBN: 0847694305.
This highly regarded short history places the Crusades within the medieval social, economic, religious, and intellectual environments that produced and sustained the movement. Includes a historiographical overview.

Crusades
by Terry Jones, Illustrated by Alan Ereira
Facts on File, 1995. Hardcover, ISBN: 0816032750
Welsh-born Terry Jones is best-known as a Monty Python, but he's also an accomplished medievalist. This companion book to the A&E documentary (see below) leans on his irreverent style to convey highlights of Crusades history with lots of color illustrations.

Crusades (DVD)
Directed by Alan Ereira and David Wallace. A & E Entertainment, 2002. Two discs, run time 200 minutes. ASIN: B00005U8F3
Jones wrote the scripts for and narrates each of the 50-minute segments of this entertaining and educational documentary, which tends to come down on the side of those who condemn the Crusades as a European imperialist adventure. Ereira co-executive-produced the series.

The Crusades and the Holy Land
by Georges Tate. Thames and Hudson Ltd (New Horizons), 1996. Paperback: ISBN: 050030064X
Also published as *The Crusaders: Warriors of God* (Abrams Discoveries), this small volume offers readable narrative and lavish illustrations. An appendix includes some primary documents on various themes. A good introduction.

The Crusades Through Arab Eyes
by Amin Maalouf. Schocken, 1980.
Paperback, ISBN: 0805208984.
The author, a novelist and journalist, uses Arab accounts of the Crusades by eyewitnesses and participants to create a well-balanced narrative of how the conflicts was (and is)

seen in the Near East. He describes the complex political/religious structures of the era, shows how conflict within the Arab world led to some Crusader successes, and offers insights into the forces that shape Arab and Islamic consciousness today.

The Dream and the Tomb
by Robert Payne. Cooper Square Publishers (reissue), 2000.
Paperback, ISBN: 0815410867.
Payne's lively prose turns history into an enthralling narrative. This comprehensive history in one volume is richly detailed, if somewhat less informed on the Muslim perspective. Small lapses in consistency don't detract from its effect.

A History of the Crusades (3 volumes)
by Steven Runciman. Cambridge University Press, 1987.
Volume 1: *The First Crusade and the Foundation of the Kingdom of Jerusalem*. Paperback, ISBN: 052134770X.
Volume 2:*The Kingdom of Jerusalem*. Paperback, ISBN:0521347718
Volume 3: *The Kingdom of Acre and the Later Crusades*. Paperback, ISBN: 0521347726
At 1,600-plus pages, Sir Steven Runciman's classic is for the serious enthusiast. Written nearly 50 years ago, it champions the viewpoint that the Crusades were motivated more by economics than true religious fervor: a view currently being challenged. But as he writes, "Whether we regard the Crusades as the most tremendous and most romantic of Christian adventures, or as the last of the barbarian invasions, they form a central fact in medieval history."

Holy War: The Crusades and Their Impact on Today's World,
by Karen Armstrong. Anchor Books, 2001.
Paperback, ISBN: 0385721404.
The bestselling religious historian sets out to prove her thesis that the persistent conflict of Christians, Jews, and Muslims in the Near East is largely a legacy of the Crusades.

John of Ibelin and the Kingdom of Jerusalem
by Peter W. Edbury. Boydell Press 1997.
Hardcover, ISBN: 0851157033.
Balian of Ibelin sprang from a prominent knightly clan of Outremer. This scholarly biography of his most famous descendant, by a leading medievalist, begins with the 12th-century Ibelins. Expensive; may be in some library collections.

The Oxford Illustrated History of the Crusades
by Jonathan Riley-Smith. Oxford University Press, 2001.
Paperback, ISBN: 0192854283.
As editor, Riley-Smith introduces this collection authored by more than a dozen specialists, who analyze the complex religious, economic, and military aspects of the Crusades. Has been called engrossing, authoritative, and comprehensive. Extensively illustrated with photos, paintings, drawings, maps, and chronologies.

Saladin and the Fall of Jerusalem
by Stanley Lane-Poole and David Nicolle. Greenhill Books, 2002. Hardcover, ISBN: 1853675032.
Classic account of Saladin and his times draws on the colorful chronicles of Muslim historians for insight into the warrior-monarch's life and deeds.

The Talisman
by Sir Walter Scott. Wildside Press, 2002.
Hardcover, ISBN: 1592247709 (other editions available).
Scott's 1825 novel centered on the clashes of England's Richard I (Lionheart) and Saladin, taking place after the events in *Kingdom of Heaven*. It epitomizes the romantic Victorian view of the Crusades and cemented the legends of Saladin's chivalry and nobility.

Acknowledgments

For their essential contributions to this book, the editor and publisher wish to thank:

At Twentieth Century Fox: Debbie Olshan, who oversaw the project from start to finish, and her assistant, Marilyn Dukala; Steve Asbell, vice president of production; Steve Newman, director, still photography, and his assistant, Laura Howe; Carol Sewell, senior vice president, publicity, and Jeffrey Godsick, executive vice president, publicity; and Fox Filmed Entertainment co-chairmen Tom Rothman and Jim Gianopulos.

At Scott Free Productions: Lisa Ellzey, executive producer of *Kingdom of Heaven*, who somehow made time to provide materials, review manuscript and layouts, and help us contact many people who worked on the film; her assistant, Shane Starr; and Jane Templeton, Ridley Scott's assistant in the London office of Scott Free.

Production heads and staff for *Kingdom of Heaven*, who shared their experience and expertise: executive producers Terry Needham and Branko Lustig, production designer Arthur Max and his talented art department, editor Dody Dorn, costume designer Janty Yates, set decorator Sonja Klaus, casting directors Jina Jay and Debbie Zane, visual effects producer Victoria Alonso, and visual effects supervisor Wes Sewell. Screenwriter William Monahan, who contributed many details and insights on the film's conception and writing process.

Unit photographer David Appleby and his associate Juliana Malucelli, for their gorgeous photographs.

At Laurizika Motion Picture Company: Charles de Lauzirika and Paul Prischman, and Shant Istamboulian at Deluxe Digital Studios, who shared visual materials while producing the *Kingdom of Heaven* DVD.

Nancy Friedman, whose research and writing for the "Lords of Outremer" chapter add so much to the book's interest and value.

At Night and Day Design: Timothy Shaner, for the brilliant book design, and Christopher Measom, for photo research.

And especially director and producer Ridley Scott, for contributing his memories, his storyboards, and his time during a hectic post-production schedule; for his generous introduction; and for the consummate artistry he brings to moviemaking.

We gratefully acknowledge permission to reprint the following copyrighted material:

Pages 12-13: Detail, *Battle of Dorylaeum*, by Gustave Doré, 1877, Plate #15; **p. 20:** Courtesy of Universal Studios Licensing LLLP; **p. 21:** © Python (Monty) Pictures Limited; **pp. 22, 28, 95** (bottom), **142-143,** and **156**: From *Encyclopédie Médiévale*, by Eugène Viollet Le Duc, Inter-Livre, Chantilly, France: reprinted August 1993; **p. 26:** Ms 5089-90 *Battle between Saracens and Christians during the Crusades*, from "Chroniques des empereurs," by David Aubert, 1462 (vellum), Brabant School, (15th century)/ Bibliothèque de L'Arsenal, Paris, France, Archives Charmet/ www.bridgeman.co.uk; **p. 30:** *Ptolemais given to Philip Augustus (1165-1223) and Richard the Lionheart* (1157-99) 13th July 1191 (oil on canvas), Blondel, Merry Joseph (1781-1853)/Chateau de Versailles, France, Giraudon/www.bridgeman.co.uk; **pp. 36-37:** *Taking of Jerusalem by the Crusaders*, 15th July 1099, 1847 (oil on canvas), Signol, Emile (1804-92)/ Chateau de Versailles, France, Giraudon/ www.bridgeman.co.uk; **p. 41:** Fr 22495 f.43 *Battle between Crusaders and Moslems,* 14th century/Bibliothèque Nationale, Paris, France/ www.bridgeman.co.uk; **pp. 80-81:** Detail, *Entry of the Crusaders into Constantinople*, by Gustave Doré, 1877, Plate #50; **p. 92:** *Pilgrims Going to Mecca*, 1861 (oil on canvas), Belly, Léon-Auguste-Adolphe (1827-77)/Musée d'Orsay, Paris, France, Lauros/Giraudon/ www.bridgeman.co.uk; **pp. 94** and **166:** Details of *Jerusalem*, by August Löffler, Inv.-Nr. 676, courtesy of Staatsgalerie Stuttgart; **p. 95** (top): Detail, *Saladin*, by Gustave Doré, 1877, Plate #38; and **p. 154:** *Guillaume de Clermont defending Ptolemais (Acre) in 1291*, 1845 (oil on canvas), Papety, Dominique Louis (1815-49)/Chateau de Versailles, France, Lauros/Giraudon/www.bridgeman.co.uk.

The publisher has made every effort to contact copyright holders; any errors or omissions are inadvertent and will be corrected upon notice in future reprintings.

The following websites provided valuable source material: For "The Reel Crusades," **pages 20-21:** "Medieval History in the Movies," www.fordham.edu/halsall/medfilms.html. For the features "Knightly Garb," **pages 142-43**, and "Beware Flying Objects," **pages 156-57**, Wikipedia, the Free Encyclopedia; en.wikipedia.org. For information on composer Harry Gregson-Williams: Cinemusic.Net, www.cinemusic.net/spotlight/1999/hgw-spotlight.html.